1/6

THE GREATEST THING IN
THE WORLD
AND OTHER ADDRESSES

Printed in Great Britain

THE GREATEST
THING IN THE WORLD

AND OTHER ADDRESSES

HENRY DRUMMOND

With an Introduction by Professor
J. Y. Simpson, D.Sc., F.R.S.E.

LONDON AND GLASGOW
COLLINS' CLEAR-TYPE PRESS

CONTENTS

PART I

PART II

PART III

CONTENTS

PART I

PART II

PART III

INTRODUCTION

HENRY DRUMMOND was born at Stirling on the
17th of August, 1851 ; he died at Tunbridge Wells
on March 11th, 1897. Consequently his life, in
the maturity of its powers, was lived through a
most distinctive period—the last quarter of last
century—when the full impact of the truth that
was in Darwin was rapidly being felt far beyond
the narrow scientific area of its first dominance,
under the sledge-hammer blows of a Huxley or
the more overwhelming torrent of the Spencerian
philosophy. The noble if placid orthodoxy of the
greater Victorian poets notwithstanding, a ferment
was at work in the minds of many of the younger
generation, which in some cases resolved itself
into a struggle between loyalty to an old theology
or to a new science that were felt to be incompatible
with one another. Realising the basal correspon-
dences and unity of the truth which could be
reached along the various highways of Revelation,
Henry Drummond, with an inherited love for,
and broadly developed interest in, Natural Science,
strove to convey to others those glimpses of a

7

wider outlook and flashes from a penetrative insight that had cheered and illumined his own too solitary path. To what an extent he had met a need of his generation may be gathered from the fact that the British sales of one of his larger works,—*Natural Law in the Spiritual World*—reached something like 130,000 copies, whilst of the addresses here published, that one which gives title to the volume had in his lifetime a circulation of 350,000 in booklet form. His writings provoked criticism in many undiscerning quarters, but it is noteworthy that one of the most distinguished of his critics, long years after, made public avowal of how completely he had failed to gauge the need for, or estimate the value of, the kind of work, viz., that on the relations of scientific and religious thought, done by Drummond. It is a need that has only become more clamant with the passage of the years.

Under the moulding influence of an ideal home life, Henry Drummond passed by way of Edinburgh University, which he entered at the age of fifteen, into New College, Edinburgh, although with no very clear idea as to how the " call " to religious service which had led him thither, might eventually be responded to in his particular case. At no time, apparently, had he ever thought of the active ministry, and his interest in his scientific studies had never slackened. The natural bent of his mind towards preoccupation with the relations of scientific and religious thought was seen in the subjects that were selected by him for class or Debating Society essays during his student days, as e.g. the " Six Days of Creation " ; " Was the Deluge Partial ? " ; " The Doctrine of Creation." Then, in the third winter of his theological studies, he was swept into the current of the great Mission conducted by Messrs. Moody and Sankey in Great Britain during 1873-1875. It was an experience in which he found himself, and in which men began to realise his extraordinary powers of expression and appeal. " There's nobody in the world like Drummond for interesting young men," Mr. Moody had said ; " set him to talk to a lot of 'em, and he'll just crop 'em in in five minutes." The Mission ended, he returned after two years' absence to the class-room benches, and quietly resumed his student place as if nothing had happened. Yet very much had happened, for while in the midst of the Mission he could say that " underlying my scientific studies and everything else, there has been this one settled conviction all these years—that the only life which to me would seem at all worth living would be a life of evangelistic work," a fuller experience had shown him that "the great thing is to *live* rather than to *work*," and that the immediate business for him now was in quietness and confidence to prepare himself spiritually for what he had no doubt would be made clear as God's purpose in life for him.

Very soon his way became clear before him. In the autumn of 1877 he applied for the vacant lectureship on Natural Science in the Free Church College, Glasgow, and helped largely by a very commendatory testimonial from Sir Archibald Geikie, whom he later accompanied on a geological expedition to the Rocky Mountains, was elected to the post. Yet even with this definite demanding work in hand, he could not neglect the gift of evangelism that was in him. "I want a quiet mission somewhere," he wrote, "entry immediate and self-contained." It was his artisan audiences in Possil Park, Glasgow, who first heard the addresses that were afterwards collected and published as *Natural Law in the Spiritual World*. When, as the result of his work, the mission at Possil Park was made into a full charge, Henry Drummond retired from that post, and an ordained minister was appointed in his place. On his return from Africa in the spring of 1884 his lectureship, to

which he had been re-appointed year by year, was
raised to the status of a Chair through the vision
and generosity of Mr. James Stevenson of Hailie,
and he, unruffled by the rapidly mounting sales of
his now famous book and the growing requests of
those who sought spiritual counsel from him, was
unanimously elected to the post by the General
Assembly of his Church. His inaugural lecture on
" The Contribution of Science to Christianity,"
when published later, added greatly to his reputation.

The year 1885 is still remembered by an older
generation as the commencement of the long and
happy association of Henry Drummond with the
student life of Edinburgh University. In the
autumn of 1884 the student world of Great Britain
was stirred by the news that Stanley Smith and
C. T. Studd, two brilliant Cambridge athletes, had
resolved, along with five of their college friends,
to devote themselves to mission work in China.
Previous to their departure, the two leaders paid
a series of farewell visits to various other Universities, and made such a deep impression in Edinburgh that they were invited to return if possible,
which they did, within two months' time. The
results were so profoundly moving that the local
leaders felt that the work must be continued. Now

it happened that in between the two visits of the Cambridge volunteers, Professor Drummond had delivered the annual lecture to the Christian Medical Association of Edinburgh University, taking as his subject " The Contribution of Science to Christianity." After that evening, when over four hundred men were captured by his presentation of old truth in a new light, it was not difficult to know who should be invited to carry on the work. Most fortunately he accepted the invitation, and for ten years, until he was stricken by the illness which proved fatal, he addressed meetings of Edinburgh University students in the Oddfellows' Hall for from four to six Sundays every spring. Of those who assisted him most, probably least will ever be known. The earlier years were particularly memorable, for small deputations of the men, headed by a professor or lecturer, visited the other Scottish Universities in turn, where, at meetings recognised by the local teaching staff, Christian Associations were formed, and the religious life of the University quickened. The resulting Holiday Mission, carefully organised under Drummond's immediate supervision, took groups of students to other towns and villages, and it is noteworthy that he made it a rule on all these occasions that the student members of the deputations should, so far as they went beyond describing the Edinburgh work, confine themselves merely to testifying to some truth that they had made their own by personal experience. In time news of the work reached far beyond Great Britain. As a result, on two occasions in the United States, in Australia, and on the Continent, Henry Drummond went by invitation from University to University and College to College, sometimes accompanied by a representative deputation of Edinburgh professors or students, proclaiming the truth as he had come to see it. There are those who still remember the thrill with which they first heard the outlines of the address on Love at a Northfield Conference, U.S.A., in the summer of 1887, although it had certainly been given some four years earlier at a mission station service in Central Africa.

To few men of science is it given to write with clarity and distinction. From an early period Henry Drummond had practised writing, and in his later years became almost fastidious about phrasing and expression. In particular he would insist on the careful selection of adjectives, a part of speech which he considered to be especially determinative of the care that a writer put into his work. So it is not surprising to learn that the original Introduction to *The Ascent of Man*, his greatest book, was, after being set up in type, entirely re-written and reduced in length as the result of a friendly criticism, or that he had a large first edition of one of his booklets suppressed just before publication, because he discovered a faulty paragraph in it at the last moment,—" a knot in the porridge," as he put it. Some may recall his mot, " *A Nineteenth Century* article should be written at least three times, once in simplicity, once in profundity, and once to make the profundity appear simplicity." Even more strongly he wrote to a young friend in 1895, " For your humility read Frederick Harrison's article in the October number of *The Nineteenth Century* on Ruskin as a Master of English Prose. After reading it you will wonder, as I did, however any of us have the face to print a line."

Concerning his message, the addresses speak for themselves. They are as vital and constraining to-day as when he first delivered them. They gripped men ; they changed lives, not for a day but for all time. " I continually meet men from the Edinburgh meetings, holding like limpets," he wrote in 1890, during his tour in Australia. And his influence abides. Enter the private office of the Chief Magistrate of the capital city of

Scotland, and the first thing that catches your eye is an enlarged photograph of Henry Drummond, and it would not be difficult to name man after man at the top of his profession to-day who would admit that one of the greatest influences for good in his life under God was Henry Drummond. This man, with something of the cavalier about him,—the students most closely associated with him in his work invariably spoke of him as " The Prince,"—with his wonderful power of literary expression, fine distinction of mind, and above all that selfless redemptive note about his life which was its key-note, eludes all efforts at portrayal. But that which he was, which he had at heart, and which was continuously exemplified in his life, may be glimpsed anew and savingly realised by another generation through his words.

J. Y. SIMPSON.

PART ONE

I.

THE GREATEST THING
IN THE WORLD

THOUGH I speak with the tongues of men and of angels, and have not Love, I am become as sounding brass, or a tinkling cymbal. And though I have the gift of prophecy, and understand all mysteries, and all knowledge ; and though I have all faith, so that I could remove mountains, and have not Love, I am nothing. And though I bestow all my goods to feed the poor, and though I give my body to be burned, and have not Love, it profiteth me nothing.

Love suffereth long, and is kind ;
Love envieth not ;
Love vaunteth not itself, is not puffed up,
Doth not behave itself unseemly,
Seeketh not her own,
Is not easily provoked,
Thinketh no evil ;
Rejoiceth not in iniquity, but rejoiceth in the truth ;
Beareth all things, believeth all things, hopeth all things, endureth all things.

*Love never faileth : but whether there be prophecies, they shall fail ; whether there be tongues, they shall cease ; whether there be knowledge, it shall vanish away. For we know in part, and we prophesy in part. But when that which is perfect is come, then that which is in part shall be done away. When I was a child, I spake as a child, I understood as a child, I thought as a child : but when I became a man, I put away childish things. For now we see through a glass, darkly ; but then face to face : now I know in part ; but then shall I know even as also I am known. And now abideth faith, hope, Love, these three ; but the greatest of these is Love.—*I COR. xiii.

THE GREATEST THING
IN THE WORLD

EVERY one has asked himself the great question of antiquity as of the modern world : What is the *summum bonum*—the supreme good ? You have life before you. Once only you can live it. What is the noblest object of desire, the supreme gift to covet ?

We have been accustomed to be told that the greatest thing in the religious world is Faith. That great word has been the key-note for centuries of the popular religion ; and we have easily learned to look upon it as the greatest thing in the world. Well, we are wrong. If we have been told that, we may miss the mark. I have taken you, in the chapter which I have just read, to Christianity at its source ; and there we have seen, " The greatest of these is love." It is not an over-sight. Paul was speaking of faith just a moment before. He says, " If I have all faith, so that I can remove mountains, and have not love, I am nothing." So far from forgetting, he deliberately contrasts them, " Now abideth Faith, Hope,

Love," and without a moment's hesitation, the decision falls, " The greatest of these is Love."

And it is not prejudice. A man is apt to recommend to others his own strong point. Love was not Paul's strong point. The observing student can detect a beautiful tenderness growing and ripening all through his character as Paul gets old ; but the hand that wrote, " The greatest of these is love," when we meet it first, is stained with blood.

Nor is this letter to the Corinthians peculiar in singling out love as the *summum bonum*. The masterpieces of Christianity are agreed about it. Peter says, " Above all things have fervent love among yourselves." *Above all things.* And John goes farther, " God is love." And you remember the profound remark which Paul makes elsewhere, " Love is the fulfilling of the law." Did you ever think what he meant by that ? In those days men were working their passage to Heaven by keeping the Ten Commandments, and the hundred and ten other commandments which they had manufactured out of them. Christ said, I will show you a more simple way. If you do one thing, you will do these hundred and ten things, without ever thinking about them. If you love, you will unconsciously fulfil the whole law. And you can readily see for yourselves how that must be so. Take any of the commandments. " Thou shalt have no other gods before Me." If a man love God, you will not require to tell him that. Love is the fulfilling of that law. " Take not His name in vain." Would he ever dream of taking His name in vain if he loved Him ? " Remember the Sabbath day to keep it holy." Would he not be too glad to have one day in seven to dedicate more exclusively to the object of his affection ? Love would fulfil all these laws regarding God. And so, if he loved Man, you would never think of telling him to honour his father and mother. He could not do anything else. It would be preposterous to tell him not to kill. You could only insult him if you suggested that he should not steal—how could he steal from those he loved ? It would be superfluous to beg him not to bear false witness against his neighbour. If he loved him it would be the last thing he would do. And you would never dream of urging him not to covet what his neighbours had. He would rather they possessed it than himself. In this way " Love is the fulfilling of the law." It is the rule for fulfilling all rules, the new commandment for keeping all the old commandments, Christ's one secret of the Christian life.

Now Paul had learned that ; and in this noble

eulogy he has given us the most wonderful and original account extant of the *summum bonum*. We may divide it into three parts. In the beginning of the short chapter, we have Love *contrasted ;* in the heart of it, we have Love *analysed ;* towards the end we have Love *defended* as the supreme gift.

THE CONTRAST

PAUL begins by contrasting Love with other things that men in those days thought much of. I shall not attempt to go over those things in detail. Their inferiority is already obvious.

He contrasts it with eloquence. And what a noble gift it is, the power of playing upon the souls and wills of men, and rousing them to lofty purposes and holy deeds. Paul says, " If I speak with the tongues of men and of angels, and have not love, I am become as sounding brass, or a tinkling cymbal." And we all know why. We have all felt the brazenness of words without emotion, the hollowness, the unaccountable unpersuasiveness, of eloquence behind which lies no Love.

He contrasts it with prophecy. He contrasts

it with mysteries. He contrasts it with faith. He contrasts it with charity. Why is Love greater than faith ? Because the end is greater than the means. And why is it greater than charity ? Because the whole is greater than the part. Love is greater than faith, because the end is greater than the means. What is the use of having faith ? It is to connect the soul with God. And what is the object of connecting man with God ? That he may become like God. But God is Love. Hence Faith, the means, is in order to Love, the end. Love, therefore, obviously is greater than faith. It is greater than charity, again, because the whole is greater than a part. Charity is only a little bit of Love, one of the innumerable avenues of Love, and there may even be, and there is, a great deal of charity without Love. It is a very easy thing to toss a copper to a beggar in the street ; it is generally an easier thing than not to do it. Yet Love is just as often in the withholding. We purchase relief from the sympathetic feelings roused by the spectacle of misery, at the copper's cost. It is too cheap—too cheap for us, and often too dear for the beggar. If we really loved him we would either do more for him, or less.

Then Paul contrasts it with sacrifice and martyrdom. And I beg the little band of would-be

missionaries—and I have the honour to call some
of you by this name for the first time—to remember
that though you give your bodies to be burned,
and have not Love, it profits nothing—nothing !
You can take nothing greater to the heathen world
than the impress and reflection of the Love of
God upon your own character. That is the universal
language. It will take you years to speak in
Chinese, or in the dialects of India. From the day
you land, that language of Love, understood by all,
will be pouring forth its unconscious eloquence.
It is the man who is the missionary, it is not his
words. His character is his message. In the heart
of Africa, among the great Lakes, I have come across
black men and women who remembered the only
white man they ever saw before—David Living-
stone ; and as you cross his footsteps in that dark
continent, men's faces light up as they speak of the
kind Doctor who passed there years ago. They
could not understand him ; but they felt the Love
that beat in his heart. Take into your new sphere
of labour, where you also mean to lay down your
life, that simple charm, and your lifework must
succeed. You can take nothing greater, you need
take nothing less. It is not worth while going if
you take anything less. You may take every
accomplishment ; you may be braced for every

sacrifice ; but if you give your body to be burned, and have not Love, it will profit you and the cause of Christ *nothing*.

THE ANALYSIS

AFTER contrasting Love with these things, Paul in three verses, very short, gives us an amazing analysis of what this supreme thing is. I ask you to look at it. It is a compound thing, he tells us. It is like light. As you have seen a man of science take a beam of light and pass it through a crystal prism, as you have seen it come out on the other side of the prism broken up into its component colours—red, and blue, and yellow, and violet, and orange, and all the colours of the rainbow— so Paul passes this thing, Love, through the magnificent prism of his inspired intellect, and it comes out on the other side broken up into its elements. And in these few words we have what one might call the Spectrum of Love, the analysis of Love. Will you observe what its elements are ? Will you notice that they have common names ; that they are virtues which we hear about every day ; that they are things which can be practised by every man in every place in life ; and how, by a multitude of small things and ordinary virtues, the supreme thing, the *summum bonum*, is made up ?

The Spectrum of Love has nine ingredients :—

Patience . .	" Love suffereth long."
Kindness . .	" And is kind."
Generosity .	" Love envieth not."
Humility . .	" Love vaunteth not itself, is not puffed up."
Courtesy . .	" Doth not behave itself unseemly."
Unselfishness	" Seeketh not her own."
Good Temper	" Is not easily provoked."
Guilelessness .	" Thinketh no evil."
Sincerity . .	" Rejoiceth not in iniquity, but rejoiceth in the truth."

Patience ; kindness ; generosity ; humility ; courtesy ; unselfishness ; good temper ; guilelessness ; sincerity—these make up the supreme gift, the stature of the perfect man. You will observe that all are in relation to men, in relation to life, in relation to the known to-day and the near to-morrow, and not to the unknown eternity. We hear much of love to God ; Christ spoke much of love to man. We make a great deal of peace with heaven ; Christ made much of peace on earth

Religion is not a strange or added thing, but the inspiration of the secular life, the breathing of an eternal spirit through this temporal world. The supreme thing, in short, is not a thing at all, but the giving of a further finish to the multitudinous words and acts which make up the sum of every common day.

There is no time to do more than make a passing note upon each of these ingredients. Love is *Patience*. This is the normal attitude of Love; Love passive, Love waiting to begin; not in a hurry; calm; ready to do its work when the summons comes, but meantime wearing the ornament of a meek and quiet spirit. Love suffers long; beareth all things; believeth all things; hopeth all things. For Love understands, and therefore waits.

Kindness. Love active. Have you ever noticed how much of Christ's life was spent in doing kind things—in *merely* doing kind things? Run over it with that in view, and you will find that He spent a great proportion of His time simply in making people happy, in doing good turns to people. There is only one thing greater than happiness in the world, and that is holiness; and it is not in our keeping; but what God *has* put in our power is the happiness of those about us, and that is largely to be secured by our being kind to them.

"The greatest thing," says some one, "a man can do for his Heavenly Father is to be kind to some of His other children." I wonder why it is that we are not all kinder than we are. How much the world needs it. How easily it is done. How instantaneously it acts. How infallibly it is remembered. How superabundantly it pays itself back—for there is no debtor in the world so honourable, so superbly honourable, as Love. "Love never faileth." Love is success, Love is happiness, Love is life. "Love, I say," with Browning, "is energy of Life."

"For life, with all it yields of joy and woe
  And hope and fear,
  Is just our chance o' the prize of learning love—
  How love might be, hath been indeed, and is."

Where Love is, God is. He that dwelleth in Love dwelleth in God. God is love. Therefore *love*. Without distinction, without calculation, without procrastination, love. Lavish it upon the poor, where it is very easy ; especially upon the rich, who often need it most ; most of all upon our equals, where it is very difficult, and for whom perhaps we each do least of all. There is a difference between *trying to please* and *giving pleasure*. Give pleasure. Lose no chance of giving pleasure. For that is the ceaseless and anonymous triumph of a truly loving spirit. " I will pass through this world but once. Any good thing therefore that I can do, or any kindness that I can show to any human being, let me do it now. Let me not defer it or neglect it, for I shall not pass this way again."

Generosity. " Love envieth not." This is Love in competition with others Whenever you attempt a good work you will find other men doing the same kind of work, and probably doing it better. Envy them not. Envy is a feeling of ill-will to those who are in the same line as ourselves, a spirit of covetousness and detraction. How little Christian work even is a protection against un-Christian feeling. That most despicable of all the unworthy moods which cloud a Christian's soul assuredly waits for us on the threshold of every work, unless we are fortified with this grace of magnanimity. Only one thing truly need the Christian envy, the large, rich, generous soul which " envieth not."

And then, after having learned all that, you have to learn this further thing, *Humility*— to put a seal upon your lips and forget what you have done. After you have been kind, after Love has stolen forth into the world and done its beautiful work, go back into the shade again and say nothing about it. Love hides even from itself. Love waives even self-satisfaction. " Love vaunteth not itself, is not puffed up."

The fifth ingredient is a somewhat strange one to find in this *summum bonum : Courtesy*. This is Love in society, Love in relation to etiquette. " Love doth not behave itself unseemly." Politeness has been defined as love in trifles. Courtesy is said to be love in little things. And the one secret of politeness is to love. Love *cannot* behave itself unseemly. You can put the most untutored person into the highest society, and if they have a reservoir of love in their heart, they will not behave themselves unseemly. They simply cannot do it. Carlyle said of Robert Burns that there was no truer gentleman in Europe than the ploughman-poet. It was because he loved everything—the mouse, and the daisy, and all the things, great and small, that God had made. So with this simple passport he could mingle with any society, and enter courts and palaces from his little cottage on the banks of the Ayr. You know the meaning of the word " gentleman." It means a gentle man—a man who does things gently, with love. And that is the whole art and mystery of it. The gentle man cannot in the nature of things do an ungentle, an ungentlemanly thing. The ungentle soul, the inconsiderate, unsympathetic nature cannot do anything else. " Love doth not behave itself unseemly."

Unselfishness. " Love seeketh not her own." Observe : Seeketh not even that which is her own. In Britain the Englishman is devoted, and rightly, to his rights. But there come times when a man may exercise even the higher right of giving up his rights. Yet Paul does not summon us to give up our rights. Love strikes much deeper. It would have us not seek them at all, ignore them, eliminate the personal element altogether from our calculations. It is not hard to give up our rights. They are often external The difficult thing is to give up ourselves. The more difficult thing still is not to seek things for ourselves at all. After we have sought them, bought them, won them, deserved them, we have taken the cream off them for ourselves already. Little cross then, perhaps, to give them up. But not to seek them, to look every man not on his own things, but on the things of others—*id opus est*. " Seekest thou great things for thyself ? " said the prophet ; " *seek them not*." Why ? Because there is no greatness in *things*. Things cannot be great. The only greatness is unselfish love. Even self-denial in itself is nothing, is almost a mistake. Only a great purpose or a mightier love can justify the waste. It is more difficult, I have said, not to seek our own at all, than, having sought it, to give it up. I must take that back. It is only true of a partly selfish heart. Nothing is a hardship to Love, and nothing is hard. I believe that Christ's yoke is easy. Christ's " yoke " is just His way of taking life. And I believe it is an easier way than any other. I believe it is a happier way than any other. The most obvious lesson in Christ's teaching is that there is no happiness in having and getting anything, but only in giving. I repeat, *there is no happiness in having, or in getting, but only in giving*. And half the world is on the wrong scent in the pursuit of happiness. They think it consists in having and getting, and in being served by others. It consists in giving and serving others. He that would be great among you, said Christ, let him serve. He that would be happy, let him remember that there is but one way—it is more blessed, it is more happy, to give than to receive.

The next ingredient is a very remarkable one : *Good Temper*. " Love is not easily provoked." Nothing could be more striking than to find this here. We are inclined to look upon bad temper as a very harmless weakness. We speak of it as a mere infirmity of nature, a family failing, a matter of temperament, not a thing to take into very serious account in estimating a man's character. And yet here, right in the heart of this analysis of love, it finds a place; and the Bible again and again returns to condemn it as one of the most destructive elements in human nature.

The peculiarity of ill temper is that it is the vice of the virtuous. It is often the one blot on an otherwise noble character. You know men who are all but perfect, and women who would be entirely perfect, but for an easily ruffled, quick-tempered, or " touchy " disposition. This compatibility of ill temper with high moral character is one of the strangest and saddest problems of ethics. The truth is there are two great classes of sins—sins of the *Body*, and sins of the *Disposition*. The Prodigal Son may be taken as a type of the first, the Elder Brother of the second. Now society has no doubt whatever as to which of these is the worse. Its brands falls, without a challenge, upon the Prodigal. But are we right ? We have no balance to weigh one another's sins, and coarser and finer are but human words ; but faults in the higher nature may be less venial than those in the lower, and to the eye of Him who is Love, a sin against Love may seem a hundred times more base. No form of vice, not worldliness, not greed of gold, not drunkenness itself, does more to un-Christianise society than evil temper. For embittering life, for breaking up communities, for destroying the most sacred relationships, for devastating homes, for withering up men and women, for taking the bloom off childhood ; in short, for sheer gratuitous misery-producing power, this influence stands alone. Look at the Elder Brother, moral, hard-working, patient, dutiful—let him get all credit for his virtues—look at this man, this baby, sulking outside his own father's door. " He was angry," we read, " and would not go in " Look at the effect upon the father. upon the servants, upon the happiness of the guests. Judge of the effect upon the Prodigal—and how many prodigals are kept out of the Kingdom of God by the unlovely characters of those who profess to be inside ? Analyse, as a study in Temper, the thunder-cloud itself as it gathers upon the Elder Brother's brow. What is it made of ? Jealousy, anger, pride, uncharity, cruelty, self-righteousness, touchiness, doggedness, sullenness—these are the ingredients of this dark and loveless soul. In vary-ing proportions, also, these are the ingredients of all ill temper. Judge if such sins of the disposition are not worse to live in, and for others to live with, than sins of the body. Did Christ indeed not

answer the question Himself when He said, " I
say unto you, that the publicans and the harlots
go into the Kingdom of Heaven before you."
There is really no place in Heaven for a disposition
like this. A man with such a mood could only make
Heaven miserable for all the people in it. Except,
therefore, such a man be born again, he cannot, he
simply *cannot*, enter the Kingdom of Heaven. For
it is perfectly certain—and you will not misunderstand me—that to enter Heaven a man must take
it with him.

You will see then why Temper is significant.
It is not in what it is alone, but in what it reveals.
This is why I take the liberty now of speaking of it
with such unusual plainness. It is a test for love, a
symptom, a revelation of an unloving nature at
bottom. It is the intermittent fever which bespeaks
unintermittent disease within ; the occasional
bubble escaping to the surface which betrays some
rottenness underneath ; a sample of the most
hidden products of the soul dropped involuntarily
when off one's guard ; in a word, the lightning
form of a hundred hideous and un-Christian sins.
For a want of patience, a want of kindness, a
want of generosity, a want of courtesy, a want of
unselfishness, are all instantaneously symbolised
in one flash of Temper.

Hence it is not enough to deal with the Temper. We must go to the source, and change the inmost nature, and the angry humours will die away of themselves. Souls are made sweet not by taking the acid fluids out, but by putting something in— a great Love, a new Spirit, the Spirit of Christ. Christ, the Spirit of Christ, interpenetrating ours, sweetens, purifies, transforms all. This only can eradicate what is wrong, work a chemical change, renovate and regenerate, and rehabilitate the inner man. Will-power does not change men. Time does not change men. Christ does. Therefore " Let that mind be in you which was also in Christ Jesus." Some of us have not much time to lose. Remember, once more, that this is a matter of life or death. I cannot help speaking urgently, for myself, for yourselves. " Whoso shall offend one of these little ones, which believe in me, it were better for him that a millstone were hanged about his neck, and that he were drowned in the depth of the sea." That is to say, it is the deliberate verdict of the Lord Jesus that it is better not to live than not to love. *It is better not to live than not to love.*

Guilelessness and *Sincerity* may be dismissed almost with a word. Guilelessness is the grace for suspicious people. And the possession of it is the great secret of personal influence. You will find, if you think for a moment, that the people who influence you are people who believe in you. In an atmosphere of suspicion men shrivel up; but in that atmosphere they expand, and find encouragement and educative fellowship. It is a wonderful thing that here and there in this hard, uncharitable world there should still be left a few rare souls who think no evil. This is the great unworldliness. Love " thinketh no evil," imputes no motive, sees the bright side, puts the best construction on every action. What a delightful state of mind to live in! What a stimulus and benediction even to meet with it for a day! To be trusted is to be saved. And if we try to influence or elevate others, we shall soon see that success is in proportion to their belief of our belief in them. For the respect of another is the first restoration of the self-respect a man has lost; our ideal of what he is becomes to him the hope and pattern of what he may become.

" Love rejoiceth not in iniquity, but rejoiceth in the truth." I have called this *Sincerity* from the words rendered in the Authorised Version by " rejoiceth in the truth." And, certainly, were this the real translation, nothing could be more just. For he who loves will love Truth not less than men. He will rejoice in the Truth—rejoice not in what he has been taught to believe; not in this

Church's doctrine or in that ; not in this ism or in
that ism ; but " in *the Truth.*" He will accept only
what is real ; he will strive to get at facts ; he
will search for *Truth* with a humble and unbiased
mind, and cherish whatever he finds at any sacrifice. But the more literal translation of the Revised
Version calls for just such a sacrifice for truth's
sake here. For what Paul really meant is, as we there
read, " Rejoiceth not in unrighteousness, but
rejoiceth with the truth," a quality which probably
no one English word—and certainly not *Sincerity*—
adequately defines. It includes, perhaps more
strictly, the self-restraint which refuses to make
capital out of others' faults ; the charity which
delights not in exposing the weakness of others,
but " covereth all things " ; the sincerity of purpose which endeavours to see things as they are,
and rejoices to find them better than suspicion
feared or calumny denounced.

So much for the analysis of Love. Now the business of our lives is to have these things fitted into
our characters. That is the supreme work to which
we need to address ourselves in this world, to learn
Love. Is life not full of opportunities for learning
Love ? Every man and woman every day has a
thousand of them. The world is not a play-ground ;
it is a school-room. Life is not a holiday, but an

education. And the one eternal lesson for us all is *how better we can love.* What makes a man a good cricketer ? Practice. What makes a man a good artist, a good sculptor, a good musician ? Practice. What makes a man a good linguist, a good stenographer ? Practice. What makes a man a good man ? Practice. Nothing else. There is nothing capricious about religion. We do not get the soul in different ways, under different laws, from those in which we get the body and the mind. If a man does not exercise his arm he develops no biceps muscle ; and if a man does not exercise his soul, he acquires no muscle in his soul, no strength of character, no vigour of moral fibre, nor beauty of spiritual growth. Love is not a thing of enthusiastic emotion. It is a rich, strong, manly, vigorous expression of the whole round Christian character. —the Christ-like nature in its fullest development. And the constituents of this great character are only to be built up by ceaseless practice.

What was Christ doing in the carpenter's shop ? Practising. Though perfect, we read that He *learned* obedience, He *increased* in wisdom and in favour with God and man. Do not quarrel therefore with your lot in life. Do not complain of its never-ceasing cares, its petty environment, the vexations you have to stand, the small and sordid

souls you have to live and work with. Above all,
do not resent temptation ; do not be perplexed
because it seems to thicken round you more and
more, and ceases neither for effort nor for agony
nor prayer. That is the practice which God appoints
you ; and it is having its work in making you
patient, and humble, and generous, and unselfish,
and kind, and courteous. Do not grudge the hand
that is moulding the still too shapeless image within
you. It is growing more beautiful though you see
it not, and every touch of temptation may add to
its perfection. Therefore keep in the midst of life.
Do not isolate yourself. Be among men, and among
things, and among troubles, and difficulties, and
obstacles. You remember Goethe's words : *Es
bildet ein Talent sich in der Stille, Doch ein Character
in dem Strom der Welt.* " Talent develops itself
in solitude ; character in the stream of life."
Talent develops itself in solitude—the talent of
prayer, of faith, of meditation, of seeing the
unseen ; Character grows in the stream of the
world's life. That chiefly is where men are to
learn love.

How ? Now, how ? To make it easier, I have
named a few of the elements of love. But these are
only elements. Love itself can never be defined.
Light is a something more than the sum of its

ingredients—a glowing, dazzling, tremulous ether.
And love is something more than all its elements—
a palpitating, quivering, sensitive, living thing.
By synthesis of all the colours, men can make
whiteness, they cannot make light. By synthesis
of all the virtues, men can make virtue, they cannot
make love. How then are we to have this transcendent living whole conveyed into our souls ?
We brace our wills to secure it. We try to copy
those who have it. We lay down rules about it.
We watch. We pray. But these things alone will
not bring Love into our nature. Love is an *effect*.
And only as we fulfil the right condition can we
have the effect produced. Shall I tell you what the
cause is ?

If you turn to the Revised Version of the First
Epistle of John you will find these words : " We
love, because He first loved us." " We love,"
not " We love *Him*. That is the way the old
Version has it, and it is quite wrong. " *We
love*—because He first loved us." Look at that
word " because." It is the *cause* of which I
have spoken. " *Because* He first loved us," the
effect follows that we love, we love Him, we love
all men. We cannot help it. Because He loved us,
we love, we love everybody. Our heart is slowly
changed. Contemplate the love of Christ, and you

will love. Stand before that mirror, reflect Christ's character, and you will be changed into the same image from tenderness to tenderness. There is no other way. You cannot love to order. You can only look at the lovely object, and fall in love with it, and grow into likeness to it. And so look at this Perfect Character, this Perfect Life. Look at the great Sacrifice as He laid down Himself, all through life, and upon the Cross of Calvary ; and you must love Him. And loving Him, you must become like Him. Love begets love. It is a process of induction. Put a piece of iron in the presence of a magnetised body, and that piece of iron for a time becomes magnetised. It is charged with an attractive force in the mere presence of the original force, and as long as you leave the two side by side, they are both magnets alike. Remain side by side with Him who loved us, and gave Himself for us, and you too will become a centre of power, a permanently attractive force ; and like Him you will draw all men unto you, like Him you will be drawn unto all men. That is the inevitable effect of Love. Any man who fulfils that cause must have that effect produced in him. Try to give up the idea that religion comes to us by chance, or by mystery, or by caprice. It comes to us by natural law, or by super-natural law, for all law is Divine. Edward Irving went to see a dying boy once, and when he entered the room he just put his hand on the sufferer's head, and said, " My boy, God loves you," and went away. And the boy started from his bed, and called out to the people in the house, " God loves me ! God loves me ! " It changed that boy. The sense that God loved him overpowered him, melted him down, and began the creating of a new heart in him. And that is how the love of God melts down the unlovely heart in man, and begets in him the new creature, who is patient and humble and gentle and unselfish. And there is no other way to get it. There is no mystery about it. We love others, we love everybody, we love our enemies, because He first loved us.

THE DEFENCE

Now I have a closing sentence or two to add about Paul's reason for singling out love as the supreme possession. It is a very remarkable reason. In a single word it is this : *it lasts*. " Love," urges Paul, " never faileth." Then he begins again one of his marvellous lists of the great things of the day, and exposes them one by one. He runs over the things that men thought were going to last, and shows that they are all fleeting, temporary, passing away.

" Whether there be prophecies, they shall fail." It was the mother's ambition for her boy in those days that he should become a prophet. For hundreds of years God had never spoken by means of any prophet, and at that time the prophet was greater than the king. Men waited wistfully for another messenger to come, and hung upon his lips when he appeared as upon the very voice of God. Paul says, " Whether there be prophecies they shall fail." This Book is full of prophecies. One by one they have " failed " ; that is, having been fulfilled their work is finished ; they have nothing more to do now in the world except to feed a devout man's faith.

Then Paul talks about tongues. That was another thing that was greatly coveted. " Whether there be tongues, they shall cease." As we all know, many centuries have passed since tongues have been known in this world. They have ceased. Take it in any sense you like. Take it, for illustration merely, as languages in general—a sense which was not in Paul's mind at all, and which though it cannot give us the specific lesson will point the general truth. Consider the words in which these chapters were written—Greek. It has gone. Take the Latin—the other great tongue of those days. It ceased long ago. Look at the Indian language. It is ceasing. The language of Wales, of Ireland, of the Scottish Highlands is dying before our eyes. The most popular book in the English tongue at the present time, except the Bible, is one of Dickens's works, his *Pickwick Papers*. It is largely written in the language of London street-life ; and experts assure us that in fifty years it will be unintelligible to the average English reader.

Then Paul goes farther, and with even greater boldness adds. " Whether there be knowledge, it shall vanish away " The wisdom of the ancients, where is it ? It is wholly gone. A schoolboy to-day knows more than Sir Isaac Newton knew. His knowledge has vanished away You put yesterday's paper in the fire. Its knowledge has vanished away. You buy the old editions of the great encyclopædias for a few pence. Their knowledge has vanished away. Look how the coach has been superseded by the use of steam. Look how electricity has superseded that, and swept a hundred almost new inventions into oblivion. One of the greatest living authorities, Sir William Thomson, said the other day, " The steam-engine is passing away."

" Whether there be knowledge, it shall vanish away." At every workshop you will see, in the back yard, a heap of old iron, a few wheels, a few levers, a few cranks, broken and eaten with rust. Twenty years ago that was the pride of the city. Men flocked in from the country to see the great invention ; now it is superseded, its day is done. And all the boasted science and philosophy of this day will soon be old. But yesterday, in the University of Edinburgh, the greatest figure in the faculty was Sir James Simpson, the discoverer of chloroform. The other day his successor and nephew, Professor Simpson, was asked by the librarian of the University to go to the library and pick out the books on his subject that were no longer needed. And his reply to the librarian was this : " Take every text book that is more than ten years old, and put it down in the cellar." Sir James Simpson was a great authority only a few years ago : men came from all parts of the earth to consult him ; and almost the whole teaching of that time is consigned by the science of to-day to oblivion. And in every branch of science it is the same. " Now we know in part. We see through a glass darkly."

Can you tell me anything that is going to last ? Many things Paul did not condescend to name.

He did not mention money, fortune, fame ; but he picked out the great things of his time, the things the best men thought had something in them, and brushed them peremptorily aside. Paul had no charge against these things in themselves. All he said about them was that they would not last. They were great things, but not supreme things. They were things beyond them. What we are stretches past what we do, beyond what we possess. Many things that men denounce as sins are not sins ; but they are temporary. And that is a favourite argument of the New Testament. John says of the world, not that it is wrong, but simply that it " passeth away." There is a great deal in the world that is delightful and beautiful ; there is a great deal in it that is great and engrossing ; but it will not last. All that is in the world, the lust of the eye, the lust of the flesh, and the pride of life, are but for a little while. Love not the world therefore. Nothing that it contains is worth the life and consecration of an immortal soul. The immortal soul must give itself to something that is immortal. And the only immortal things are these : " Now abideth faith, hope, love, but the greatest of these is love."

Some think the time will come when two of these three things will also pass away—faith into

sight, hope into fruition. Paul does not say so.
We know but little now about the conditions of the
life that is to come. But what is certain is that Love
must last. God, the Eternal God, is Love. Covet
therefore that everlasting gift, that one thing
which it is certain is going to stand, that one coinage
which will be current in the Universe when all the
other coinages of all the nations of the world shall
be useless and unhonoured. You will give yourselves to many things, give yourselves first to Love.
Hold things in their proportion. *Hold things in
their proportion*. Let at least the first great object
of our lives be to achieve the character defended
in these words, the character,—and it is the
character of Christ—which is built round Love.

I have said this thing is eternal. Did you ever
notice how continually John associates love and
faith with eternal life ? I was not told when I was
a boy that " God so loved the world that He
gave His only begotten Son, that whosoever
believeth in Him should have everlasting life."
What I was told, I remember, was, that God
so loved the world that, if I trusted in Him,
I was to have a thing called peace, or I was
to have rest, or I was to have joy, or I was to have
safety. But I had to find out for myself that whosoever trusteth in Him—that is, whosoever loveth

Him, for trust is only the avenue to Love—hath
everlasting *life*. The Gospel offers a man life.
Never offer men a thimbleful of Gospel. Do not
offer them merely joy, or merely peace, or merely
rest, or merely safety ; tell them how Christ came
to give men a more abundant life than they have,
a life abundant in love, and therefore abundant
in salvation for themselves, and large in enterprise
for the alleviation and redemption of the world.
Then only can the Gospel take hold of the whole
of a man, body, soul, and spirit, and give to each
part of his nature its exercise and reward. Many of
the current Gospels are addressed only to a part of
man's nature. They offer peace, not life ; faith, not
Love ; justification, not regeneration. And men
slip back again from such religion because it has
never really held them. Their nature was not all
in it. It offered no deeper and gladder life-current
than the life that was lived before. Surely it
stands to reason that only a fuller love can compete
with the love of the world.

To love abundantly is to live abundantly, and
to love for ever is to live for ever. Hence, eternal
life is inextricably bound up with love. We want
to live for ever for the same reason that we want
to live to-morrow. Why do you want to live
to-morrow ? It is because there is some one who

loves you, and whom you want to see to-morrow, and be with, and love back. There is no other reason why we should live on than that we love and are beloved. It is when a man has no one to love him that he commits suicide. So long as he has friends, those who love him and whom he loves, he will live ; because to live is to love. Be it but the love of a dog, it will keep him in life ; but let that go and he has no contact with life, no reason to live. The " energy of life " has failed. Eternal life also is to know God, and God is love. This is Christ's own definition. Ponder it. " This is life eternal, that they might know Thee the only true God, and Jesus Christ whom Thou hast sent." Love must be eternal. It is what God is. On the last analysis, then, love is Life. Love never faileth, and life never faileth, so long as there is love. That is the philosophy of what Paul is showing us ; the reason why in the nature of things Love should be the supreme thing—because it is going to last ; because in the nature of things it is an Eternal Life. That Life is a thing that we are living now, not that we get when we die ; that we shall have a poor chance of getting when we die unless we are living now. No worse fate can befall a man in this world than to live and grow old alone, unloving and un-loved. To be lost is to live in an unregenerate

condition, loveless and unloved ; and to be saved is
to love ; and he that dwelleth in love dwelleth
already in God. For God is love.

Now I have all but finished. How many of you
will join me in reading this chapter once a week for
the next three months ? A man did that once and
it changed his whole life. Will you do it ? It is for
the greatest thing in the world. You might begin
by reading it every day, especially the verses
which describe the perfect character. " Love
suffereth long, and is kind ; love envieth not ;
love vaunteth not itself." Get these ingredients
into your life. Then everything that you do is
eternal. It is worth doing. It is worth giving time
to. No man can become a saint in his sleep ;
and to fulfil the condition required demands a
certain amount of prayer and meditation and time,
just as improvement in any direction, bodily or
mental, requires preparation and care. Address
yourself to that one thing ; at any cost have this
transcendent character exchanged for yours. You
will find as you look back upon your life that the
moments that stand out, the moments when you
have really lived, are the moments when you
have done things in a spirit of love. As memory
scans the past, above and beyond all the transitory
pleasures of life, there leap forward those supreme

hours when you have been enabled to do unnoticed kindnesses to those around about you, things too trifling to speak about, but which you feel have entered into your eternal life. I have seen almost all the beautiful things that God has made; I have enjoyed almost every pleasure that He has planned for man; and yet as I look back I see standing out above all the life that has gone four or five short experiences when the love of God reflected itself in some poor imitation, some small act of love of mine, and these seem to be the things which alone of all one's life abide. Everything else in all our lives is transitory. Every other good is visionary. But the acts of love which no man knows about, or can ever know about—they never fail.

In the Book of Matthew, where the Judgment Day is depicted for us in the imagery of One seated upon a throne and dividing the sheep from the goats, the test of a man then is not, "How have I believed?" but "How have I loved?" The test of religion, the final test of religion, is not religiousness, but Love. I say the final test of religion at that great Day is not religiousness, but Love; not what I have done, not what I have believed, not what I have achieved, but how I have discharged the common charities of life. Sins of commission in that awful indictment are not even referred to. By what we have not done, *by sins of omission*, we are judged. It could not be otherwise. For the withholding of love is the negation of the spirit of Christ, the proof that we never knew Him, that for us He lived in vain. It means that He suggested nothing in all our thoughts, that He inspired nothing in all our lives, that we were not once near enough to Him to be seized with the spell of His compassion for the world. It means that :

> " I lived for myself, I thought for myself,
> For myself, and none beside—
> Just as if Jesus had never lived,
> As if He had never died."

It is the Son of *Man* before whom the nations of the world shall be gathered. It is in the presence of *Humanity* that we shall be charged. And the spectacle itself, the mere sight of it, will silently judge each one. Those will be there whom we have met and helped ; or there, the unpitied multitude whom we neglected or despised. No other Witness need be summoned. No other charge than lovelessness shall be preferred. Be not deceived. The words which all of us shall one Day hear, sound not of theology but of life, not of churches and saints

but of the hungry and the poor, not of creeds and
doctrines but of shelter and clothing, not of
Bibles and prayer-books but of cups of cold water
in the name of Christ. Thank God the Christianity
of to-day is coming nearer the world's need. Live
to help that on. Thank God men know better, by a
hairsbreadth, what religion is, what God is, who
Christ is, where Christ is. Who is Christ? He who
fed the hungry, clothed the naked, visited the sick.
And where is Christ? Where?—whoso shall receive
a little child in My name receiveth Me. And who are
Christ's? Every one that loveth is born of God.

PART TWO

PART TWO

II.
THE
PROGRAMME OF CHRISTIANITY

To Preach Good Tidings unto the Meek :
To Bind up the Broken-Hearted :
To Proclaim Liberty to the Captives and the Opening
of the Prison to Them that are Bound :
To Proclaim the Acceptable Year of the Lord, and
the Day of Vengeance of our God :
To Comfort all that Mourn :
To Appoint unto them that Mourn in Zion :
To Give unto them—
Beauty for Ashes,
The Oil of Joy for Mourning,
The Garment of Praise for the Spirit of Heaviness.

THE
PROGRAMME OF CHRISTIANITY

" WHAT does God do all day ? " once asked a
little boy. One could wish that more grown-up
people would ask so very real a question. Unfor-
tunately, most of us are not even boys in religious
intelligence, but only very unthinking children.
It no more occurs to us that God is engaged in
any particular work in the world than it occurs
to a little child that its father does anything except
be its father. Its father may be a Cabinet Minister
absorbed in the nation's work, or an inventor deep
in schemes for the world's good ; but to this master-
egoist he is father, and nothing more. Childhood,
whether in the physical or moral world, is the great
self-centred period of life ; and a personal God
who satisfies personal ends is all that for a long time
many a Christian understands.

But as clearly as there comes to the growing
child a knowledge of its father's part in the world,
and a sense of what real life means, there must
come to every Christian whose growth is true some

richer sense of the meaning of Christianity and a larger view of Christ's purpose for mankind. To miss this is to miss the whole splendour and glory of Christ's religion. Next to losing the sense of a personal Christ, the worst evil that can befall a Christian is to have no sense of anything else. To grow up in complacent belief that God has no business in this great groaning world of human beings except to attend to a few saved souls is the negation of all religion. The first great epoch in a Christian's life, after the awe and wonder of its dawn, is when there breaks into his mind some sense that Christ has a purpose for mankind, a purpose beyond him and his needs, beyond the churches and their creeds, beyond Heaven and its saints—a purpose which embraces every man and woman born, every kindred and nation formed, which regards not their spiritual good alone but their welfare in every part, their progress, their health, their work, their wages, their happiness in this present world.

What, then, does Christ do all day ? By what further conception shall we augment the selfish view of why Christ lived and died ?

I shall mislead no one, I hope, if I say—for I wish to put the social side of Christianity in its strongest light—that Christ did not come into the world to give men religion. He never mentioned the word religion. Religion was in the world before Christ came, and it lives to-day in a million souls who have never heard His name. *What God does all day* is not to sit waiting in churches for people to come and worship Him. It is true that God is in churches and in all kinds of churches, and is found by many in churches more immediately than anywhere else. It is also true that while Christ did not give men religion He gave a new direction to the religious aspiration bursting forth then and now and always from the whole world's heart. But it was His purpose to enlist these aspirations on behalf of some definite practical good. The religious people of those days did nothing with their religion except attend to its observances. Even the priest, after he been to the temple, thought his work was done ; when he met the wounded man he passed by on the other side. Christ reversed all this—tried to reverse it, for He is only now beginning to succeed. The tendency of the religions of all time has been to care more for religion than for humanity ; Christ cared more for humanity than for religion—rather His care for humanity was the chief expression of His religion. He was not indifferent to observances, but the practices of the people bulked in His thoughts before the practices of the Church. It has been pointed out as a blemish on the immortal allegory of Bunyan that the Pilgrim never *did* anything, anything but save his soul. The remark is scarcely fair, for the allegory is designedly the story of a soul in a single relation; and, besides, he did do a little. But the warning may well be weighed. The Pilgrim's one thought, his work by day, his dream by night, was *escape*. He took little part in the world through which he passed. He was a *Pilgrim* travelling through it ; his business was to get through safe. Whatever this is, it is not Christianity. Christ's conception of Christianity was heavens removed from that of a man setting out from the City of Destruction to save his soul. It was rather that of a man dwelling amidst the Destructions of the City and planning escapes for the souls of others—escapes not to the other world, but to purity and peace and righteousness in this. In reality Christ never said " Save your soul." It is a mistranslation which says that. What He said was, " Save your life." And this not because the first is nothing, but only because it is so very great a thing that only the second can accomplish it. But the new word altruism—the translation of " love thy neighbour as thyself "— is slowly finding its way into current Christian speech. The People's Progress, not less than the

Pilgrim's Progress, is daily becoming a graver concern to the Church. A popular theology with unselfishness as part at least of its root, a theology which appeals no longer to fear, but to the generous heart in man, has already dawned, and more clearly than ever men are beginning to see what Christ really came into this world to do.

What Christ came here for was to make a better world. The world in which we live is an unfinished world. It is not wise, it is not happy, it is not pure, it is not good—it is not even sanitary. Humanity is little more than raw material. Almost everything has yet to be done to it. Before the days of Geology people thought the earth was finished. It is by no means finished. The work of Creation is going on. Before the spectroscope, men thought the universe was finished. We know now it is just beginning. And this teeming universe of men in which we live has almost all its finer colour and beauty yet to take. Christ came to complete it. The fires of its passions were not yet cool ; their heat had to be transformed into finer energies. The ideals for its future were all to shape, the forces to realise them were not yet born. The poison of its sins had met no antidote, the gloom of its doubt no light, the weight of its sorrow no rest. These the Saviour of the world, the Light of men, would do and be. This, roughly, was His scheme.

Now this was a prodigious task—to recreate the world. How was it to be done ? God's way of making worlds is to make them make themselves. When He made the earth He made a rough ball of matter and supplied it with a multitude of tools to mould it into form—the rain-drop to carve it, the glacier to smooth it, the river to nourish it, the flower to adorn it. God works always with agents, and this is our way when we want any great thing done, and this was Christ's way when He undertook the finishing of Humanity. He had a vast intractable mass of matter to deal with, and He required a multitude of tools. Christ's tools were men. Hence His first business in the world was to make a collection of men. In other words He founded a Society.

THE FOUNDING OF THE SOCIETY

It is a somewhat startling thought—it will not be misunderstood—that Christ probably did not save many people while He was here. Many an evangelist in that direction has done much more. He never intended to finish the world single-handed, but announced from the first that others would not only take part, but do " greater things " than He. For amazing as was the attention He was able to give to individuals, this was not the whole aim He had in view. His immediate work was to enlist men in His enterprise, to rally them into a great company or Society for the carrying out of His plans.

The name by which this Society was known was *The Kingdom of God.* Christ did not coin this name ; it was an old expression, and good men had always hoped and prayed that some such Society would be born in their midst. But it was never either defined or set agoing in earnest until Christ made its realisation the passion of His life.

How keenly He felt regarding His task, how enthusiastically He set about it, every page of His life bears witness. All reformers have one or two great words which they use incessantly, and by mere reiteration imbed indelibly in the thought and history of their time. Christ's great word was the Kingdom of God. Of all the words of His that have come down to us this is by far the commonest. One hundred times it occurs in the Gospels. When He preached He had almost always this for a text. His sermons were explanations of the aims of His Society, of the different things it was like, of whom its membership consisted, what they were to do or to be, or not do or not be. And even when He does not actually use the word, it is easy to see that all He said and did had reference to this. Philosophers talk about thinking in categories— the mind living, as it were, in a particular room with its own special furniture, pictures, and view-points, these giving a consistent direction and colour to all that is there thought or expressed. It was in the category of the Kingdom that Christ's thought moved. Though one time He said He came to save the lost, or at another time to give men life, or to do His Father's will, these were all included among the objects of His Society.

No one can ever know what Christianity is till he has grasped this leading thought in the mind of Christ. Peter and Paul have many wonderful and necessary things to tell us about what Christ was and did ; but we are looking now at what Christ's own thought was. Do not think this is a mere modern theory. These are His own life-plans taken from His own lips. Do not allow any isolated text, even though it seem to sum up for you the Christian life, to keep you from trying to understand Christ's Programme as a whole. The perspective of Christ's teaching is not everything, but without it every-thing will be distorted and untrue. There is much good in a verse, but often much evil. To see some small soul pirouetting throughout life on a single text, and judging all the world because it cannot find a partner, is not a Christian sight. Christianity does not grudge such souls their comfort. What it grudges is that they make Christ's Kingdom uninhabitable to thoughtful minds. Be sure that whenever the religion of Christ appears small, or forbidding, or narrow, or inhuman, you are dealing not with the whole—which is a matchless moral symmetry—nor even with an arch or column—for every detail is perfect—but with some cold stone removed from its place and suggesting nothing of the glorious structure from which it came.

Tens of thousands of persons who are familiar with religious truths have not noticed yet that Christ ever founded a Society at all. The reason is partly that people have read texts instead of reading their Bible, partly that they have studied Theology instead of studying Christianity, and partly because of the noiselessness and invisibility of the Kingdom of God itself. Nothing truer was ever said of this Kingdom than that " It cometh without observation." Its first discovery, therefore, comes to the Christian with all the force of a revelation. The sense of belonging to such a Society transforms life. It is the difference between being a solitary knight tilting single-handed, and often defeated, at whatever enemy one chances to meet on one's little acre of life, and the *feel* of belonging to a mighty army marching throughout all time to a certain victory. This note of universality given to even the humblest work we do, this sense of comradeship, this link with history, this thought of a definite campaign, this promise of success, is the possession of every obscurest unit in the Kingdom of God.

THE PROGRAMME OF THE SOCIETY

HUNDREDS of years before Christ's Society was formed, its Programme had been issued to the world. I cannot think of any scene in history more dramatic than when Jesus entered the church in Nazareth and read it to the people. Not that when He appropriated to Himself that venerable fragment from Isaiah He was uttering a manifesto or announcing His formal Programme. Christ never did things formally. We think of the words, as He probably thought of them, not in their old-world historical significance, nor as a full expression of His future aims, but as a summary of great moral facts now and always to be realised in the world since he appeared.

Remember as you read the words to what grim reality they refer. Recall what Christ's problem really was, what His Society was founded for. This Programme deals with a real world. Think of it as you read—not of the surface-world, but of the world as it is, as it sins and weeps, and curses and suffers and sends up its long cry to God. Limit it if you like to the world around your door, but think of it—of the city and the hospital and the dungeon and the graveyard, of the sweating-shop and the pawn-shop and the drink-shop ; think of the cold, the cruelty, the fever, the famine, the ugliness, the loneliness, the pain. And then try to keep down the lump in your throat as you take up His Programme and read—

To Bind up the Broken-Hearted :
To Proclaim Liberty to the Captives :
To Comfort all that Mourn :
To Give unto them—
    Beauty for Ashes,
    The Oil of Joy for Mourning,
    The Garment of Praise for the Spirit of
    Heaviness.

What an exchange—Beauty for Ashes, Joy for Mourning, Liberty for Chains! No marvel " the eyes of all them that were in the synagogue were fastened on Him " as He read ; or that they " wondered at the gracious words which proceeded out of His lips." Only one man in that congregation, only one man in the world to-day could hear these accents with dismay—the man, the culprit, who has said hard words of Christ.

We are all familiar with the protest, " Of course " —as if there were no other alternative to a person of culture—" Of course I am not a Christian, but I always speak *respectfully* of Christianity." Respectfully of Christianity! No remark fills one's soul with such sadness. One can understand a man as he reads these words being stricken speechless ; one can see the soul within him rise to a white heat as each fresh benediction falls upon his ear and drives him, a half-mad enthusiast, to bear them to the world. But in what school has he learned of Christ who offers the Saviour of the world his respect ?

Men repudiate Christ's religion because they think it a small and limited thing, a scheme with no large human interests to commend it to this great social age. I ask you to note that there is not one burning interest of the human race which is not

represented here. What are the great words of
Christianity according to this Programme ! Take
as specimens these :

LIBERTY,

COMFORT,

BEAUTY,

JOY.

These are among the greatest words of life. Give
them their due extension, the significance which
Christ undoubtedly saw in them and which
Christianity undoubtedly yields, and there is almost
no great want or interest of mankind which they do
not cover.

These are not only the greatest words of life, but
they are the best. This Programme, to those who
have misread Christianity, is a series of surprises.
Observe the most prominent note in it. It is
gladness. Its first word is " good-tidings," its last
is " joy." The saddest words of life are also there—
but there as the diseases which Christianity comes
to cure. No life that is occupied with such an
enterprise could be other than radiant. The contribution of Christianity to the joy of the living,
perhaps even more to the joy of *thinking*, is un-
speakable. The joyful life is the life of the larger
mission, the disinterested life, the life of the over-
flow from self, the " more abundant life " which

comes from following Christ. And the joy of thinking is the larger thinking, the thinking of the man
who holds in his hand some Programme for
Humanity. The Christian is the only man who has
any Programme at all—any Programme either for
the world or for himself. Goethe, Byron, Carlyle
taught Humanity much, but they had no Programme for it. Byron's thinking was suffering ;
Carlyle's despair. Christianity alone exults The
belief in the universe as moral, the interpretation
of history as progress, the faith in good as eternal,
in evil as self-consuming, in humanity as evolving—
these Christian ideas have transformed the malady
of thought into a bounding hope. It was no senti-
ment but a conviction matured amid calamity and
submitted to the tests of life that inspired the
great modern poet of optimism to proclaim :

" Gladness be with thee, Helper of the world !
  I think this is the authentic sign and seal
  Of Godship, that ever waxes glad,
  And more glad, until gladness blossoms, bursts
  Into a rage to suffer for mankind
  And recommence at sorrow."

But that is not all. Man's greatest needs are often
very homely. And it is almost as much in its

fearless recognition of the commonplace woes of life, and its deliberate offerings to minor needs, that the claims of Christianity to be a religion for Humanity stand. Look, for instance, at the closing sentence of this Programme. Who would have expected to find among the special objects of Christ's solicitude the *Spirit of Heaviness* ? Supreme needs, many and varied, had been already dealt with on this Programme ; many applicants had been met ; the list is about to close. Suddenly the writer remembers the nameless malady of the poor—that mysterious disease which the rich share but cannot alleviate, which is too subtle for doctors, too incurable for Parliaments, too unpicturesque for philanthropy, too common even for sympathy. Can Christ meet that ?

If Christianity could even deal with the world's Depression, could cure mere dull spirits, it would be the Physician of Humanity. But it can. It has the secret, a hundred secrets, for the lifting of the world's gloom. It cannot immediately remove the physiological causes of dulness—though obedience to its principles can do an infinity to prevent them, and its inspirations can do even more to lift the mind above them. But where the causes are moral or mental or social, the remedy is in every Christian's hand. Think of any one at this moment whom the

Spirit of Heaviness haunts. You think of a certain old woman. But you know for a fact that you can cure her. You did so, perfectly, only a week ago. A mere visit, and a little present, or the visit without any present, set her up for seven long days, and seven long nights. The machinery of the Kingdom is very simple and very silent, and the most silent parts do most, and we all believe so little in the medicines of Christ that we do not know what ripples of healing are set in motion when we simply smile on one another. Christianity wants nothing so much in the world as sunny people, and the old are hungrier for love than for bread, and the Oil of Joy is very cheap, and if you can help the poor on with a Garment of Praise, it will be better for them than blankets.

Or perhaps you know someone else who is dull—not an old woman this time but a very rich and important man. But you also know perfectly what makes him dull. It is either his riches or his importance. Christianity can cure either of these —though you may not be the person to apply the cure—at a single hearing. Or here is a third case, one of your own servants. It is a case of *monotony*. Prescribe more variety, leisure, recreation—anything to relieve the wearing strain. A fourth case— your most honoured guest : Condition—leisure,

health, accomplishments, means; Disease—
Spiritual Obesity; Treatment—talent to be put
out to usury. And so on down the whole range of
life's dejection and *ennui*.

Perhaps you tell me this is not Christianity at
all; that everybody could do that. The curious
thing is that everybody does not. Good-will
to men came into the world with Christ, and where-
ever that is found, in Christian or heathen land,
there Christ is, and there His spirit works. And if
you say that the chief end of Christianity is not the
world's happiness, I agree; it was never meant to
be; but the strange fact is that, without making it
its chief end, it wholly and infallibly, and quite
universally, leads to it. Hence the note of Joy,
though not the highest on Christ's Programme, is
a loud and ringing note, and none who serve in His
Society can be long without its music. Time was
when a Christian used to apologise for being happy.
But the day has always been when he ought to
apologise for being miserable.

Christianity, you will observe, really works.
And it succeeds not only because it is divine, but
because it is so very human—because it is common-
sense. Why should the Garment of Praise destroy
the Spirit of Heaviness? Because an old woman
cannot sing and cry at the same moment. The

Society of Christ is a sane Society. Its methods are rational. The principle in the old woman's case is simply that one emotion destroys another. Christianity works, as a railway man would say, with points. It switches souls from valley lines to mountain lines, not stemming the currents of life but diverting them. In the rich man's case the principle of cure is different, but it is again principle, not necromancy. His spirit of heaviness is caused, like any other heaviness, by the earth's attraction. Take away the earth and you take away the attraction. But if Christianity can do anything it can take away the earth. By the wider extension of the horizon which it gives, by the new standard of values, by the mere setting of life's small pomps and interests and admirations in the light of the Eternal, it dissipates the world with a breath. All that tends to abolish worldliness tends to abolish unrest, and hence, in the rush of modern life, one far-reaching good of all even commonplace Christian preaching, all Christian literature, all which holds the world doggedly to the idea of a God and a future life, and reminds mankind of Infinity and Eternity.

Side by side with these influences, yet taking the world at a wholly different angle, works another great Christian force. How many opponents of religion are aware that one of the specific objects of Christ's Society is Beauty ? The charge of vulgarity against Christianity is an old one. If it means that Christianity deals with the ruder elements in human nature, it is true, and that is its glory. But if it means that it has no respect for the finer qualities, the charge is baseless. For Christianity not only encourages whatsoever things are lovely, but wars against that whole theory of life which would exclude them. It prescribes æstheticism. It proscribes asceticism. And for those who preach to Christians that in these enlightened days they must raise the masses by giving them noble sculptures and beautiful paintings and music and public parks, the answer is that these things are all already being given, and given daily, and with an increasing sense of their importance, by the Society of Christ. Take away from the world the beautiful things which have not come from Christ and you will make it poorer scarcely at all. Take away from modern cities the paintings, the monuments, the music for the people, the museums and the parks which are not the gifts of Christian men and Christian municipalities, and in ninety cases out of a hundred you will leave them unbereft of so much as a well-shaped lamp-post.

It is impossible to doubt that the Decorator of

the World shall not continue to serve to His later children, and in ever finer forms, the inspirations of beautiful things. More fearlessly than he has ever done, the Christian of modern life will use the noble spiritual leverages of Art. That this world, the people's world, is a bleak and ugly world, we do not forget ; it is ever with us. But we esteem too little the mission of beautiful things in haunting the mind with higher thoughts and begetting the mood which leads to God. Physical beauty makes moral beauty. Loveliness does more than destroy ugliness ; it destroys matter. A mere touch of it in a room, in a street, even on a door knocker, is a spiritual force. Ask the working-man's wife, and she will tell you there is a moral effect even in a clean table-cloth. If a barrel-organ in a slum can but drown a curse, let no Christian silence it. The mere light and colour of the wall-advertisements are a gift of God to the poor man's sombre world.

One Christmas-time a poor drunkard told me that he had gone out the night before to take his usual chance of the temptations of the street. Close to his door, at a shop window, an angel—so he said—arrested him. It was a large Christmas-card, a glorious white thing with tinsel wings, and as it glittered in the gas-light it flashed into his soul a sudden thought of Heaven. It recalled the earlier heaven of his infancy, and he thought of his mother in the distant glen, and how it would please her if she got this Christmas angel from her prodigal. With money already pledged to the devil he bought the angel, and with it a new soul and future for himself. That was a real angel. For that day as I saw its tinsel pinions shine in his squalid room I knew what Christ's angels were. They are all beautiful things, which daily in common homes are bearing up heavy souls to God.

But do not misunderstand me. This angel was made of pasteboard : a pasteboard angel can never save a soul. Tinsel reflects the sun, but warms nothing. Our Programme must go deeper. Beauty may arrest the drunkard, but it cannot cure him.

It is here that Christianity asserts itself with a supreme individuality. It is here that it parts company with Civilisation, with Politics, with all secular schemes of Social Reform. In its diagnosis of human nature it finds that which most other systems ignore ; which, if they see, they cannot cure ; which, left undestroyed, makes every reform futile, and every inspiration vain. That thing is *Sin*. Christianity, of all other philanthropies, recognises that man's devouring need is *Liberty*— liberty to stop sinning ; to leave the prison of his passions, and shake off the fetters of his past. To surround *Captives* with statues and pictures, to offer *Them-that-are-Bound* a higher wage or a cleaner street or a few more cubic feet of air per head, is solemn trifling. It is a cleaner soul they want ; a purer air, or any air at all, for their higher selves.

And where the cleaner soul is to come from apart from Christ I cannot tell. " By no political alchemy," Herbert Spencer tells us, " can you get golden conduct out of leaden instincts." The power to set the heart right, to renew the springs of action, comes from Christ. The sense of the infinite worth of the single soul, and the recoverableness of man at his worst, are the gifts of Christ. The freedom from guilt, the forgiveness of sins, come from Christ's Cross ; the hope of immortality springs from Christ's grave. We believe in the gospel of better laws and an improved environment ; we hold the religion of Christ to be a social religion ; we magnify and call Christian the work of reformers, statesmen, philanthropists, educators, inventors, sanitary officers, and all who directly or remotely aid, abet, or further the higher progress of mankind ; but in Him alone, in the fulness of that word, do we see the Saviour of the world.

There are earnest and gifted lives to-day at work

among the poor whose lips at least will not name the name of Christ. I speak of them with respect ; their shoe-latchets many of us are not worthy to unloose. But because the creed of the neighbouring mission-hall is a travesty of religion they refuse to acknowledge the power of the living Christ to stop man's sin, of the dying Christ to forgive it. O, narrowness of breadth ! Because there are ignorant doctors do I yet rail at medicine or start an hospital of my own ? Because the poor raw evangelist, or the narrow ecclesiastic, offer their little all to the poor, shall I repudiate all they do not know of Christ because of the little that they do know ? Of gospels for the poor which have not some theory, state it how you will, of personal conversion one cannot have much hope. Personal conversion means for life a personal religion, a personal trust in God, a personal debt to Christ, a personal dedication to His cause. These, brought about how you will, are supreme things to aim at, supreme losses if they are missed. Sanctification will come to masses only as it comes to individual men ; and to work with Christ's Programme and ignore Christ is to utilise the sun's light without its energy.

But this is not the only point at which the uniqueness of this Society appears. There is yet another depth in humanity which no other system

even attempts to sound. We live in a world not
only of sin but of sorrow—

" There is no flock, however watched and tended,
    But one dead lamb is there ;
There is no home, howe'er defended,
    But has one vacant chair."

When the flock thins, and the chair empties, who
is to be near to heal ? At that moment the gospels
of the world are on trial. In the presence of death
how will they act ? Act ! They are blotted out
of existence. Philosophy, Politics, Reforms, are
no more. The Picture Galleries close. The Sculptures hide. The Committees disperse. There is
crape on the door ; the world withdraws. Observe,
it withdraws. It has no mission.

So awful in its loneliness was this hour that the
Romans paid a professional class to step in with
its mummeries and try to fill it. But that is Christ's
own hour. Next to Righteousness the greatest word
of Christianity is Comfort. Christianity has almost
a monopoly of Comfort. Renan was never nearer
the mark than when he spoke of the Bible as " the
great Book of the Consolation of Humanity."
Christ's Programme is full of Comfort, studded with
Comfort : " to bind up the Broken-Hearted, to

Comfort all that mourn, to Give unto them that mourn in Zion." Even the " good tidings " to the " meek " are, in the Hebrew, a message to the " afflicted " or " the poor." The word Gospel itself comes down through the Greek from this very passage, so that whatever else Christ's Gospel means it is first an Evangel for suffering men.

One note in this Programme jars with all the rest. When Christ read from Isaiah that day He never finished the passage. A terrible word, Vengeance, yawned like a precipice across His path ; and in the middle of a sentence " He closed the Book, and gave it again to the minister, and sat down." A Day of Vengeance from our God— these were the words before which Christ paused. When the prophet proclaimed it some great historical fulfilment was in his mind. Had the people to whom Christ read been able to under-stand its ethical equivalents He would probably have read on. For, so understood, instead of filling the mind with fear, the thought of this Dread Day inspires it with a solemn gratitude. The work of the Avenger is a necessity. It is part of God's philanthropy.

For I have but touched the surface in speaking of the sorrow of the world as if it came from people dying. It comes from people living. Before ever the Broken-Hearted can be healed a hundred greater causes of suffering than death must be destroyed. Before the Captive can be free a vaster prison than his own sins must be demolished. There are hells on earth into which no breath of heaven can ever come ; these must be swept away. There are social soils in which only unrighteousness can flourish ; these must be broken up.

And that is the work of the Day of Vengeance. When is that day ? It is now. Who is the Avenger ? Law. What Law ? Criminal Law, Sanitary Law, Social Law, Natural Law. Wherever the poor are trodden upon or tread upon one another ; wherever the air is poison and the water foul ; wherever want stares, and vice reigns, and rags rot—there the Avenger takes his stand. Whatever makes it more difficult for the drunkard to reform, for the children to be pure, for the widow to earn a wage, for any of the wheels of progress to revolve—with these he deals. Delay him not. He is the messenger of Christ. Despair of him not, distrust him not. His Day dawns slowly, but his work is sure. Though evil stalks the world, it is on the way to execution ; though wrong reigns, it must end in self-combustion. The very nature of things is God's Avenger ; the very story of civilisation is the history of Christ's Throne.

Anything that prepares the way for a better social state is the fit work of the followers of Christ. Those who work on the more spiritual levels leave too much unhonoured the slow toil of multitudes of unchurched souls who prepare the material or moral environments without which these higher labours are in vain. Prevention is Christian as well as cure ; and Christianity travels sometimes by the most circuitous paths. It is given to some to work for immediate results, and from year to year they are privileged to reckon up a balance of success. But these are not always the greatest in the Kingdom of God. The men who get no stimulus from any visible reward, whose lives pass while the objects for which they toil are still too far away to comfort them ; the men who hold aloof from dazzling schemes and earn the misunderstanding of the crowd because they foresee remoter issues, who even oppose a seeming good because a deeper evil lurks beyond—these are the *statesmen* of the Kingdom of God.

THE MACHINERY OF THE SOCIETY

SUCH in dimmest outline is the Programme of
Christ's Society. Did you know that all this was
going on in the world ? Did you know that Christianity was such a living and purpose-like thing ?
Look back to the day when that Programme was
given, and you will see that it was not merely written
on paper. Watch the drama of the moral order
rise up, scene after scene, in history. Study the
social evolution of humanity, the spread of
righteousness, the amelioration of life, the freeing of
slaves, the elevation of woman, the purification of
religion, and ask what these can be if not the coming
of the Kingdom of God on earth. For it is precisely
through the movements of nations and the lives
of men that this Kingdom comes. Christ might
have done all this work Himself, with His own
hands. But He did not. The crowning wonder of
His scheme is that he entrusted it to *men*. It is the
supreme glory of humanity that the machinery for
its redemption should have been placed within
itself. I think the saddest thing in Christ's life
was that after founding a Society with aims so
glorious He had to go away and leave it.

But in reality He did not leave it. The old theory

that God made the world, made it as an inventor would make a machine, and then stood looking on to see it work, has passed away. God is no longer a remote spectator of the natural world, but immanent in it, pervading matter by His present Spirit, and ordering it by His Will. So Christ is immanent in men. His work is to move the hearts and inspire the lives of men, and through such hearts to move and reach the world. Men, only men, can carry out this work. This humanness, this inwardness, of the Kingdom is one reason why some scarcely see that it exists at all. We measure great movement by the loudness of their advertisement, or the place their externals fill in the public eye. This Kingdom has no externals. The usual methods of propagating a great cause were entirely discarded by Christ. The sword He declined ; money He had none ; literature He never used ; the Church disowned Him ; the State crucified Him. Planting His ideals in the hearts of a few poor men, He started them out unheralded to revolutionise the world. They did it by making friends—and by making enemies ; they went about, did good, sowed seed, died,and lived again in the lives of those they helped. These in turn, a fraction of them, did the same. They met, they prayed, they talked of Christ, they loved, they went among other men, and by act and word passed on their secret. The machinery of the Kingdom of God is purely social. It acts, not by commandment, but by contagion ; not by fiat, but by friendship. " The Kingdom of God is like unto leaven, which a woman took and hid in three measures of meal till the whole was leavened."

After all, like all great discoveries once they are made, this seems absolutely the most feasible method that could have been devised. Men *must* live among men. Men *must* influence men. Organisations, institutions, churches, have too much rigidity for a thing that is to flood the world. The only fluid in the world is man. War might have won for Christ's cause a passing victory ; wealth might have purchased a superficial triumph ; political power might have gained a temporary success. But in these there is no note of universality, of solidarity, of immortality. To live through the centuries and pervade the uttermost ends of the earth, to stand while kingdoms tottered and civilisations changed, to survive fallen churches and crumbling creeds—there was no soil for the Kingdom of God like the hearts of common men. Some who have written about this Kingdom have emphasised its moral grandeur, others its universality, others its adaptation to man's needs. One great writer speaks of its prodigious originality, another chiefly notices its success. I confess what almost strikes me most is the miracle of its simplicity.

Men, then, are the only means God's Spirit has of accomplishing His purpose. What men ? You. Is it worth doing, or is it not ? Is it worth while joining Christ's Society or is it not ? What do *you* do all day ? What is your personal stake in the coming of the Kingdom of Christ on earth ? You are not interested in religion, you tell me ; you do not care for your " soul." It was not about your religion I ventured to ask, still less about your soul. That you have no religion, that you do not care for your soul, does not absolve you from caring for the world in which you live. But you do not believe in this church, you reply, or accept this doctrine, or that. Christ does not, in the first instance, ask your thoughts, but your work. No man has a right to postpone his *life* for the sake of his thoughts. Why ? Because this **is** a real world, not a *think* world. Treat it as a real world—act. Think by all means, but think also of what is actual, of what like the stern world is, of how much even you, creedless and churchless, could do to make it better. The thing to be anxious about is not to be right with man, but with mankind. And, so far as I know, there is nothing so on all fours with mankind as Christianity.

There are versions of Christianity, it is true, which no self-respecting mind can do other than disown—versions so hard, so narrow, so unreal, so super-theological, that practical men can find in them neither outlet for their lives nor resting-place for their thoughts. With these we have nothing to do. With these Christ had nothing to do—except to oppose them with every word and act of His life. It too seldom occurs to those who repudiate Christianity because of its narrowness or its un-practicalness, its sanctimoniousness or its dulness, that these were the very things which Christ strove against and unweariedly condemned. It was the one risk of His religion being given to the common people—an inevitable risk which He took without reserve—that its infinite lustre should be tarnished in the fingering of the crowd or have its great truths narrowed into mean and unworthy moulds as they passed from lip to lip. But though the crowd is the object of Christianity, it is not its custodian. Deal with the Founder of this great Commonwealth Himself. Any man of honest purpose who will take the trouble to inquire at first hand what Christianity really is, will find it a thing he cannot get away from. Without either argument or pressure by the mere practicalness of its aims and the pathos of its compassions, it forces its august claim upon every serious life.

He who joins this Society finds himself in a large place. The Kingdom of God is a Society of the best men, working for the best ends, according to the best methods. Its membership is a multitude whom no man can number ; its methods are as various as human nature ; its field is the world. It is a Commonwealth, yet it honours a King ; it is a Social Brotherhood, but it acknowledges the Fatherhood of God. Though not a Philosophy the world turns to it for light ; though not Political it is the incubator of all great laws. It is more human than the State, for it deals with deeper needs ; more Catholic than the Church, for it includes whom the Church rejects. It is a Propaganda, yet it works not by agitation but by ideals. It is a Religion, yet it holds the worship of God to be mainly the service of man. Though not a Scientific Society its watchword is Evolution ; though not an Ethic it possesses the Sermon on the Mount. This mysterious Society owns no wealth but distributes fortunes. It has no minutes for history keeps them ; no member's roll for no one could make it. Its entry-money is nothing ; its subscription, all you have. The Society never

meets and it never adjourns. Its law is one word
—loyalty ; its Gospel one message—love. Verily
" Whosoever will lose his life for My sake shall find
it."

The Programme for the other life is not out yet.
For this world, for these faculties, for his one short
life, I know nothing that is offered to man to com-
pare with membership in the Kingdom of God.
Among the mysteries which compass the world
beyond, none is greater than how there can be in
store for man a work more wonderful, a life more
God-like than this. If you know anything better,
live for it ; if not, in the name of God and of
Humanity, carry out Christ's plan.

PART THREE

PART THREE

PAX VOBISCUM

Come unto Me all ye that are weary and heavy-laden And I will give you Rest

Take My Yoke upon you and learn of Me, for I am Meek and Lowly in heart, and ye shall find Rest unto your souls. For My Yoke is easy and My Burden light.

PAX VOBISCUM

INTRODUCTORY

I HEARD the other morning a sermon by a distinguished preacher upon " Rest." It was full of delightful thoughts ; but when I came to ask myself, " How does he say I can get Rest ? " there was no answer. The sermon was sincerely meant to be practical, yet it contained no experience that seemed to me to be tangible, nor any advice which could help me to find the thing itself as I went about the world that afternoon. Yet this omission of the only important problem was not the fault of the preacher. The whole popular religion is in the twilight here. And when pressed for really working specifics for the experiences with which it deals, it falters, and seems to lose itself in mist.

This want of connection between the great words of religion and every-day life has bewildered and discouraged all of us. Christianity possesses the noblest words in the language ; its literature overflows with terms expressive of the greatest and happiest moods which can fill the soul of man.

Rest, Joy, Peace, Faith, Love, Light—these words occur with such persistency in hymns and prayers that an observer might think they formed the staple of Christian experience. But on coming to close quarters with the actual life of most of us, how surely would he be disenchanted. I do not think we ourselves are aware how much our religious life is made up of phrases; how much of what we call Christian experience is only a dialect of the Churches, a mere religious phraseology with almost nothing behind it in what we really feel and know.

To some of us, indeed, the Christian experiences seem further away than when we took the first steps in the Christian life. That life has not opened out as we had hoped; we do not regret our religion, but we are disappointed with it. There are times, perhaps, when wandering notes from a diviner music stray into our spirits; but these experiences come at few and fitful moments. We have no sense of possession in them. When they visit us, it is a surprise. When they leave us, it is without explanation. When we wish their return, we do not know how to secure it.

All which points to a religion without solid base, and a poor and flickering life. It means a great bankruptcy in those experiences which give

Christianity its personal solace and make it attractive to the world, and a great uncertainty as to any remedy. It is as if we knew everything about health—except the way to get it.

I am quite sure that the difficulty does not lie in the fact that men are not in earnest. This is simply not the fact. All around us Christians are wearing themselves out in trying to be better. The amount of spiritual longing in the world— in the hearts of unnumbered thousands of men and women in whom we should never suspect it ; among the wise and thoughtful ; among the young and gay, who seldom assuage and never betray their thirst—this is one of the most wonderful and touching facts of life. It is not more heat that is needed, but more light ; not more force, but a wiser direction to be given to very real energies already there.

What Christian experience wants is *thread*, a vertebral column, method. It is impossible to believe that there is no remedy for its unevenness and dishevelment, or that the remedy is a secret. The idea, also, that some few men, by happy chance or happier temperament, have acquired the secret—as if there were some sort of knack or trick of it—is wholly incredible. Religion must ripen its fruit for men of every temperament ; and the way even into its highest heights must be by a gateway through which the peoples of the world may pass.

I shall try to lead up to this gateway by a very familiar path. But as that path is strangely unfrequented, and even unknown where it passes into the religious sphere, I must dwell for a moment on the commonest of commonplaces.

EFFECTS REQUIRE CAUSES

NOTHING that happens in the world happens by chance. God is a God of order. Everything is arranged upon definite principles, and never at random. The world, even the religious world, is governed by law. Character is governed by law. Happiness is governed by law. The Christian experiences are governed by law. Men, forgetting this, expect Rest, Joy, Peace, Faith, to drop into their souls from the air like snow or rain. But in point of fact they do not do so ; and if they did they would no less have their origin in previous activities and be controlled by natural laws. Rain and snow do drop from the air, but not without a long previous history. They are the mature effects of former causes. Equally so are Rest, and Peace, and Joy. They, too, have each a previous history. Storms and winds and calms are not accidents, but are brought about by antecedent circumstances. Rest and Peace are but calms in man's inward nature, and arise through causes as definite and as inevitable.

Realise it thoroughly : it is a methodical not an accidental world. If a housewife turns out a good cake, it is the result of a sound receipt, carefully applied. She cannot mix the assigned ingredients and fire them for the appropriate time without producing the result. It is not she who has made the cake ; it is nature. She brings related things together ; sets causes at work ; these causes bring about the result. She is not a creator, but an intermediary. She does not expect random causes to produce specific effects—random ingredients would only produce random cakes. So it is in the making of Christian experiences. Certain lines are followed ; certain effects are the result. These effects cannot but be the result. But the result can never take place without the previous cause. To expect results without antecedents is to expect cakes without ingredients. That impossibility is precisely the almost universal expectation. Now what I mainly wish to do is to help you to firmly grasp this simple principle of Cause and

Effect in the spiritual world. And instead of applying the principle generally to each of the Christian experiences in turn, I shall examine its application to one in some little detail. The one I shall select is Rest. And I think anyone who follows the application in this single instance will be able to apply it for himself to all the others.

Take such a sentence as this : African explorers are subject to fevers which cause restlessness and delirium. Note the expression, " cause restlessness." *Restlessness has a cause.* Clearly, then, anyone who wished to get rid of restlessness would proceed at once to deal with the cause. If that were not removed, a doctor might prescribe a hundred things, and all might be taken in turn, without producing the least effect. Things are so arranged in the original planning of the world that certain effects must follow certain causes, and certain causes must be abolished before certain effects can be removed. Certain parts of Africa are inseparably linked with the physical experience called fever ; this fever is in turn infallibly linked with a mental experience called restlessness and delirium. To abolish the mental experience the radical method would be to abolish the physical experience, and the way of abolishing the physical experience would be to abolish Africa, or to cease to go there. Now this holds good for all other forms of Restlessness. Every other form and kind of Restlessness in the world has a definite cause, and the particular kind of Restlessness can only be removed by removing the allotted cause.

All this is also true of Rest. Restlessness has a cause : Must not *Rest* have a cause ? Necessarily. If it were a chance world we would not expect this ; but, being a methodical world, it cannot be otherwise. Rest, physical rest, moral rest, spiritual rest, every kind of rest has a cause, as certainly as restlessness. Now causes are discriminating. There is one kind of cause for every particular effect, and no other ; and if one particular effect is desired, the corresponding cause must be set in motion. It is no use proposing finely devised schemes, or going through general pious exercises in the hope that somehow Rest will come. The Christian life is not casual but causal. All nature is a standing protest against the absurdity of expecting to secure spiritual effects, or any effects, without the employment of appropriate causes. The Great Teacher dealt what ought to have been the final blow to this infinite irrelevancy by a single question, "Do men gather grapes of thorns or figs of thistles?"

Why, then, did the Great Teacher not educate His followers fully ? Why did He not tell us, for example, how such a thing as Rest might be obtained ? The answer is, that *He did*. But plainly, explicitly, in so many words ? Yes, plainly, explicitly, in so many words. He assigned Rest to its cause, in words with which each of us has been familiar from our earliest childhood.

He begins, you remember—for you at once know the passage I refer to—almost as if Rest could be had without any cause : " Come unto Me," He says, " and I will *give* you Rest."

Rest, apparently, was a favour to be bestowed ; men had but to come to Him ; He would give it to every applicant. But the next sentence takes that all back. The qualification, indeed, is added instantaneously. For what the first sentence seemed to give was next thing to an impossibility. For how, in a literal sense, can Rest be *given* ? One could no more give away Rest than he could give away Laughter. We speak of " causing " laughter, which we can do ; but we cannot give it away. When we speak of giving pain, we know perfectly well we cannot give pain away. And when we aim at giving pleasure, all that we do is to arrange a set of circumstances in such a way as that these shall cause pleasure. Of course there is a sense, and a very wonderful sense, in which a Great Personality breathes upon all who come within its influence an abiding peace and trust. Men can be to other men as the shadow of a great rock in a thirsty land. Much more Christ; much more Christ as Perfect Man; much more still as Saviour of the world. But it is not this of which I speak. When Christ said He would give men Rest, He meant simply that He would put them in the way of it. By no act of conveyance would, or could, He make over His own Rest to them. He could give them His receipt for it. That was all. But He would not make it for them; for one thing, it was not in His plan to make it for them; for another thing, men were not so planned that it could be made for them; and for yet another thing, it was a thousand times better that they should make it for themselves.

That this is the meaning becomes obvious from the wording of the second sentence: " Learn of Me and ye shall *find* Rest." Rest, that is to say, is not a thing that can be given, but a thing to be *acquired*. It comes not by an act, but by a process. It is not to be found in a happy hour, as one finds a treasure; but slowly, as one finds knowledge. It could indeed be no more found in a moment than could knowledge. A soil has to be prepared for it. Like a fine fruit, it will grow in one climate and not in another; at one altitude and not at another. Like all growths it will have an orderly development and mature by slow degrees.

The nature of this slow process Christ clearly defines when He says we are to achieve Rest by *learning*. " Learn of Me," He says, " and ye shall find rest to your souls." Now consider the extraordinary originality of this utterance. How novel the connection between these two words, " Learn " and " Rest " ? How few of us have ever associated them—ever thought that Rest was a thing to be learned ; ever laid ourselves out for it as we would to learn a language ; ever practised it as we would practise the violin. Does it not show how entirely new Christ's teaching still is to the world, that so old and threadbare an aphorism should still be so little applied ? The last thing most of us would have thought of would have been to associate *Rest* with *Work*.

What must one work at ? What is that which if duly learned will find the soul of man in Rest ? Christ answers without the least hesitation. He specifies two things—Meekness and Lowliness. " Learn of Me," He says, " for I am *meek* and *lowly* in heart." Now these two things are not chosen at random. To these accomplishments, in a special way, Rest is attached. Learn these, in short, and you have already found Rest. These as they stand are direct causes of Rest ; will produce it at once; cannot but produce it at once. And if you think for a single moment, you will see how this is necessarily so, for causes are never arbitrary, and the connection between antecedent and consequent here and everywhere lies deep in the nature of things.

What is the connection, then ? I answer by a further question. What are the chief causes of *Unrest* ? If you know yourself, you will answer Pride, Selfishness, Ambition. As you look back upon the past years of your life, is it not true that its unhappiness has chiefly come from the succession of personal mortifications and almost trivial disappointments which the intercourse of life has brought you ? Great trials come at lengthened intervals, and we rise to breast them ; but it is the petty friction of our every-day life with one another, the jar of business or of work, the discord of the domestic circle, the collapse of our ambition, the crossing of our will, the taking down of our conceit, which make inward peace impossible. Wounded vanity, then, disappointed hopes, unsatisfied selfishness—these are the old, vulgar, universal sources of man's unrest.

Now it is obvious why Christ pointed out as the two chief objects for attainment the exact opposites of these. To Meekness and Lowliness these things simply do not exist. They cure unrest by making it impossible. These remedies do not trifle with surface symptoms ; they strike at once at removing causes. The ceaseless chagrin of a self-centered life can be removed at once by learning Meekness and Lowliness of heart. He who learns them is for ever proof against it. He lives henceforth a charmed life. Christianity is a fine inoculation, a transfusion of healthy blood into an anæmic or poisoned soul. No fever can attack a perfectly sound body ; no fever of unrest can disturb a soul which has breathed the air or learned the ways of Christ. Men sigh for the wings of a dove that they may fly away and be at Rest. But flying away will not help us. " The Kingdom of God is *within you.*" We aspire to the top to look for Rest ; it lies at the bottom. Water rests only when it gets to the lowest place. So do men. Hence, be lowly. The man who has no opinion of himself at all can never be hurt if others do not acknowledge him. Hence, be meek. He who is without expectation cannot fret if nothing comes to him. It is self-evident that these things are so. The lowly man and the meek man are really above all other men, above all other things. They dominate the world because they do not care for it. The miser does not possess gold, gold possesses him. But the meek possess it. " The meek," said Christ, " inherit the earth." They do not buy it ; they do not conquer it ; but they inherit it.

There are people who go about the world looking out for slights, and they are necessarily miserable, for they find them at every turn—especially the imaginary ones. One has the same pity for such men as for the very poor. They are the morally illiterate. They have had no real education, for they have never learned how to live. Few men know how to live. We grow up at random, carrying into mature life the merely animal methods and motives which we had as little children. And it does not occur to us that all this must be changed ; that much of it must be reversed ; that life is the finest of the Fine Arts ; that it has to be learned with lifelong patience, and that the years of our pilgrimage are all too short to master it triumphantly.

Yet this is what Christianity is for—to teach men the Art of Life. And its whole curriculum lies in one word—" Learn of Me." Unlike most education, this is almost purely personal ; it is not to be had from books or lectures or creeds or doctrines. It is a study from the life. Christ never said much in mere words about the Christian graces. He lived them, He was them. Yet we do not merely copy Him. We learn His art by living with Him, like the old apprentices with their masters.

Now we understand it all ? Christ's invitation to the weary and heavy-laden is a call to begin life over again upon a new principle—upon His own principle. " Watch My way of doing things," He says. " Follow Me. Take life as I take it. Be meek and lowly and you will find Rest."

I do not say, remember, that the Christian life to every man, or to any man, can be a bed of roses. No educational process can be this. And perhaps if some men knew how much was involved in the simple " learn " of Christ, they would not enter His school with so irresponsible a heart. For there is not only much to learn, but much to un-learn. Many men never go to this school at all till their disposition is already half ruined and character has taken on its fatal set. To learn arith-metic is difficult at fifty—much more to learn Christianity. To learn simply what it is to be meek and lowly, in the case of one who has had no lessons in that in childhood, may cost him half of what he values most on earth. Do we realise, for instance, that the way of teaching humility is generally by *humiliation* ? There is probably no other school for it. When a man enters himself as a pupil in such a school it means a very great thing. There is much Rest there, but there is also much Work.

I should be wrong, even though my theme is the brighter side, to ignore the cross and minimise the cost. Only it gives to the cross a more definite meaning, and a rarer value, to connect it thus directly and *causally* with the growth of the inner life. Our platitudes on the " benefits of affliction " are usually about as vague as our theories of Christian Experience. " Somehow," we believe affliction does us good. But it is not a question of " Somehow." The result is definite, calculable, necessary. It is under the strictest law of cause and effect. The first effect of losing one's fortune, for instance, is humiliation ; and the effect of humiliation, as we have just seen, is to make one humble ; and the effect of being humble is to produce Rest. It is a round-about way, apparently, of producing Rest ; but Nature generally works by circular processes ; and it is not certain that there is any other way of becoming humble, or of finding Rest. If a man could make himself humble to order, it might simplify matters, but we do not find that this happens. Hence we must all go through the mill. Hence death, death to the lower self, is the nearest gate, and the quickest road to life.

G.T.W.   H

Yet this is only half the truth. Christ's life outwardly was one of the most troubled lives that was ever lived : Tempest and tumult, tumult and tempest, the waves breaking over it all the time till the worn body was laid in the grave. But the inner life was a sea of glass. The great calm was always there. At any moment you might have gone to Him and found Rest. And even when the blood-hounds were dogging Him in the streets of Jerusalem, He turned to His disciples and offered them, as a last legacy, " My peace." Nothing ever for a moment broke the serenity of Christ's life on earth. Misfortune could not reach him ; He had no for-tune. Food, raiment, money—fountain-heads of half the world's weariness—He simply did not care for ; they played no part in His life ; He " took no thought " for them. It was impossible to affect Him by lowering His reputation ; He had already made Himself of no reputation. He was dumb before insult. When He was reviled He reviled not again. In fact, there was nothing that the world could do to Him that could ruffle the surface of His spirit.

Such living, as mere living, is altogether unique. It is only when we see what it was in Him that we can know what the word Rest means. It lies not in emotions, nor in the absence of emotions. It is

not a hallowed feeling that comes over us in church.
It is not something that the preacher has in his
voice. It is not in nature, nor in poetry, nor in
music—though in all these there is soothing. It is
the mind at leisure from itself. It is the perfect
poise of the soul; the absolute adjustment of the
inward man to the stress of all outward things;
the preparedness against every emergency; the
stability of assured convictions; the eternal calm
of an invulnerable faith; the repose of a heart set
deep in God. It is the mood of the man who says,
with Browning, "God's in His Heaven, all's well
with the world."

Two painters each painted a picture to illustrate
his conception of rest. The first chose for his
scene a still, lone lake among the far-off mountains.
The second threw on his canvas a thundering water-
fall, with a fragile birch-tree bending over the foam;
at the fork of a branch, almost wet with the
cataract's spray, a robin sat on its nest. The first
was only *Stagnation;* the last was *Rest.* For in
Rest there are always two elements—tranquillity
and energy; silence and turbulence; creation and
destruction; fearlessness and fearfulness. This it
was in Christ.

It is quite plain from all this that whatever else
He claimed to be or to do, He at least knew how

to live. All this is the perfection of living, of living in the mere sense of passing through the world in the best way. Hence His anxiety to communicate His idea of life to others. He came, He said, to give men life, true life, a more abundant life than they were living ; " the life," as the fine phrase in the Revised Version has it, " that is life indeed." This is what He himself possessed, and it was this which He offers to all mankind. And hence His direct appeal for all to come to Him who had not made much of life, who were weary and heavy-laden. These He would teach His secret. They, also, should know " the life that is life indeed."

WHAT YOKES ARE FOR

THERE is still one doubt to clear up. After the statement, " Learn of Me," Christ throws in the disconcerting qualification, " *Take My yoke* upon you and learn of Me." Why, if all this be true, does He call it a *yoke* ? Why, while professing to give Rest, does He with the next breath whisper " *burden* " ? Is the Christian life after all, what its enemies take it for—an additional weight to the already great woe of life, some extra punctiliousness about duty, some painful devotion to observances, some heavy restriction and trammelling of all that is joyous and free in the world ? Is life not hard and sorrowful enough without being fettered with yet another yoke ?

It is astounding how so glaring a misunderstanding of this plain sentence should ever have passed into currency. Did you ever stop to ask what a yoke is really for ? Is it to be a burden to the animal which wears it ? It is just the opposite. It is to make its burden light. Attached to the oxen in any other way than by a yoke, the plough would be intolerable. Worked by means of a yoke, it is light. A yoke is not an instrument of torture ; it is an instrument of mercy. It is not a malicious contrivance for making work hard ; it is a gentle device to make hard labour light. It is not meant to give pain, but to save pain. And yet men speak of the yoke of Christ as if it were a slavery, and look upon those who wear it as objects of compassion ? For generations we have had homilies on " The Yoke of Christ," some delighting in portraying its narrow exactions ; some seeking in these exactions the marks of its divinity ; others apologising for it, and toning it down ; still others assuring us that, although it be very bad, it is not to be compared with the positive blessings of

Christianity. How many, especially among the young, has this one mistaken phrase driven for ever away from the kingdom of God? Instead of making Christ attractive, it makes Him out a task-master, narrowing life by petty restrictions, calling for self-denial where none is necessary, making misery a virtue under the plea that it is the yoke of Christ, and happiness criminal because it now and then evades is. According to this conception, Christians are at best the victims of a depressing fate ; their life is a penance ; and their hope for the next world purchased by a slow martyrdom in this.

The mistake has arisen from taking the word " yoke " here in the same sense as in the expressions " under the yoke," or " wear the yoke in his youth." But in Christ's illustration it is not the *jugum* of the Roman soldier, but the simple " harness " or " ox-collar " of the Eastern peasant. It is the literal wooden yoke which He, with His own hands in the carpenter's shop, had probably often made. He knew the difference between a smooth yoke and a rough one, a bad fit and a good fit ; the difference also it made to the patient animal which had to wear is. The rough yoke galled, and the burden was heavy ; the smooth yoke caused no pain, and the load was lightly drawn. The badly fitted

harness was a misery ; the well fitted collar was
" easy."

And what was the " burden " ? It was not some
special burden laid upon the Christian, some unique
infliction that he alone must bear. It was what all
men bear. It was simply life, human life itself,
the general burden of life which all must carry with
them from the cradle to the grave. Christ saw that
men took life painfully. To some it was a weariness,
to others a failure, to many a tragedy, to all a
struggle and a pain. How to carry this burden of
life had been the whole world's problem. It is
still the whole world's problem. And here is
Christ's solution : " Carry it as I do. Take life
as I take it. Look at it from My point of view.
Interpret it upon My principles. Take My yoke
and learn of Me, and you will find it easy. For My
yoke is easy, works easily, sits right upon the
shoulders, and *therefore* My burden is light."

There is no suggestion here that religion will
absolve any man from bearing burdens. That would
be to absolve him from living, since it is life itself
that is the burden. What Christianity does propose
is to make it tolerable. Christ's yoke is simply
His secret for the alleviation of human life, His
prescription for the best and happiest method of
living. Men harness themselves to the work and

stress of the world in clumsy and unnatural ways. The harness they put on is antiquated. A rough, ill-fitted collar at the best, they make its strain and friction past enduring, by placing it where the neck is most sensitive ; and by mere continuous irritation this sensitiveness increases until the whole nature is quick and sore.

This is the origin, among other things, of a disease called " touchiness "—a disease which, in spite of its innocent name, is one of the gravest sources of restlessness in the world. Touchiness, when it becomes chronic, is a morbid condition of the inward disposition. It is self-love inflamed to the acute point ; conceit, *with a hair-trigger*. The cure is to shift the yoke to some other place ; to let men and things touch us through some new and perhaps as yet unused part of our nature ; to become meek and lowly in heart while the old nature is becoming numb from want of use. It is the beautiful work of Christianity everywhere to adjust the burden of life to those who bear it, and them to it. It has a perfectly miraculous gift of healing. Without doing any violence to human nature it sets it right with life, harmonising it with all surrounding things, and restoring those who are jaded with the fatigue and dust of the world to a new grace of living. In the mere matter of altering the perspective of life

and changing the proportions of things, its function
in lightening the care of man is altogether its own.
The weight of a load depends upon the attraction
of the earth. But suppose the attraction of the
earth were removed ? A ton on some other planet,
where the attraction of gravity is less, does not
weigh half a ton. Now Christianity removes the
attraction of the earth, and this is one way in which
it diminishes men's burden. It makes them citizens
of another world. What was a ton yesterday is
not half a ton to-day. So, without changing one's
circumstances, merely by offering a wider horizon
and a different standard, it alters the whole aspect
of the world.

Christianity as Christ taught it is the truest
philosophy of life ever spoken. But let us be quite
sure when we speak of Christianity that we mean
Christ's Christianity. Other versions are either
caricatures, or exaggerations, or misunderstandings,
or short-sighted and surface readings. For the most
part their attainment is hopeless and the results
wretched. But I care not who the person is, or
through what vale of tears he has passed, or is
about to pass, there is a new life for him along this
path.

HOW FRUITS GROW

WERE Rest my subject, there are other things I should wish to say about it, and other kinds of Rest of which I should like to speak. But that is not my subject. My theme is that the Christian experiences are not the work of magic, but come under the law of Cause and Effect. And I have chosen Rest only as a single illustration of the working of that principle. If there were time I might next run over all the Christian experiences in turn, and show how the same wide law applies to each. But I think it may serve the better purpose if I leave this further exercise to yourselves. I know no Bible study that you will find more full of fruit, or which will take you nearer to the ways of God, or make the Christian life itself more solid or more sure. I shall add only a single other illustration of what I mean, before I close.

Where does Joy come from ? I knew a Sunday scholar whose conception of Joy was that it was a thing made in lumps and kept somewhere in Heaven, and that when people prayed for it, pieces were somehow let down and fitted into their souls. I am not sure that views as gross and material are not often held by people who ought to be

wiser. In reality, Joy is as much a matter of
Cause and Effect as pain. No one can get Joy by
merely asking for it. It is one of the ripest fruits
of the Christian life, and, like all fruits, must be
grown. There is a very clever trick in India called
the mango-trick. A seed is put in the ground and
covered up, and after divers incantations a full-
blown mango-bush appears within five minutes.
I never met anyone who knew how the thing was
done, but I never met anyone who believed it to
be anything else than a conjuring-trick. The world
is pretty unanimous now in its belief in the orderli-
ness of Nature. Men may not know how fruits
grow, but they do know that they cannot grow in
five minutes. Some lives have not even a stalk on
which fruits could hang, even if they did grow in
five minutes. Some have never planted one sound
seed of Joy in all their lives ; and others who may
have planted a germ or two have lived so little in
sunshine that they never could come to maturity.

Whence, then, is Joy ? Christ put His teaching
upon this subject into one of the most exquisite
of His parables. I should in any instance have
appealed to His teaching here, as in the case of
Rest, for I do not wish you to think I am speaking
words of my own. But it so happens that He has
dealt with it in a passage of unusual fulness.

I need not recall the whole illustration. It is the parable of the Vine. Did you ever think why Christ spoke that parable? He did not merely throw it into space as a fine illustration of general truths. It was not simply a statement of the mystical union, and the doctrine of an indwelling Christ. It was that; but it was more. After He had said it, He did what was not an unusual thing when He was teaching His greatest lessons. He turned to the disciples and said He would tell them why He had spoken it. It was to tell them how to get Joy. " These things have I spoken unto you," He said, " that My joy might remain in you and that your Joy might be full." It was a purposed and deliberate communication of His secret of Happiness.

Go back over these verses, then, and you will find the Causes of this Effect, the spring, and the only spring, out of which true Happiness comes. I am not going to analyse them in detail. I ask you to enter into the words for yourselves. Remember, in the first place, that the Vine was the Eastern symbol of Joy. It was its fruit that made glad the heart of man. Yet, however innocent that gladness—for the expressed juice of the grape was the common drink at every peasant's board—the gladness was only a gross and passing thing. This was not true happiness, and the vine of the Palestine vineyards was not the true vine. *Christ* was " the *true* Vine." Here, then, is the ultimate source of Joy. Through whatever media it reaches us, all true Joy and Gladness find their source in Christ. By this, of course, is not meant that the actual Joy experienced is transferred from Christ's nature, or is something passed on from Him to us. What is passed on is His method of getting it. There is, indeed, a sense in which we can share another's joy or another's sorrow. But that is another matter. Christ is the source of Joy to men in the sense in which He is the source of rest. His people share His life, and therefore share its consequences, and one of these is Joy. His method of living is one that in the nature of things produces Joy. When He spoke of His Joy remaining with us He meant in part that the causes which produced it should continue to act. His followers, that is to say, by *repeating* His life would experience its accompaniments. His Joy, His kind of Joy, would remain with them.

The medium through which this Joy comes is next explained : " He that abideth in Me the same bringeth forth much fruit." Fruit first, Joy next ; the one the cause or medium of the other. Fruit-bearing is the necessary antecedent ; Joy both the necessary consequent and the necessary accompaniment. It lies partly in the bearing fruit, partly in the fellowship which makes that possible. Partly that is to say, Joy lies in mere constant living in Christ's presence, with all that that implies of peace, of shelter, and of love ; partly in the influence of that Life upon mind and character and will ; and partly in the inspiration to live and work for others, with all that that brings of self-riddance and Joy in other's gain. All these, in different ways and at different times, are sources of pure Happiness. Even the simplest of them —to do good to other people—is an instant and infallible specific. There is no mystery about Happiness whatever. Put in the right ingredients and it must come out. He that abideth in Him will bring forth much fruit ; and bringing forth much fruit is Happiness. The infallible receipt for Happiness, then, is to do good ; and the infallible receipt for doing good is to abide in Christ. The surest proof that all this is a plain matter of Cause and Effect is that men may try every other conceivable way of finding Happiness, and they will fail. Only the right cause in each case can produce the right effect.

Then the Christian experiences are our own making ? In the same sense in which grapes are our own making, and no more. All fruits *grow*—whether they grow in the soil or in the soul; whether they are the fruits of the wild grape or of the True Vine. No man can *make* things grow. He can *get them to grow* by arranging all the circumstances and fulfilling all the conditions. But the growing is done by God. Causes and effects are eternal arrangements, set in the constitution of the world; fixed beyond man's ordering. What man can do is to place himself in the midst of a chain of sequences. Thus he can get things to grow: thus he himself can grow. But the grower is the Spirit of God.

What more need I add but this—test the method by experiment. Do not imagine that you have got these things because you know how to get them. As well try to feed upon a cookery book. But I think I can promise that if you try in this simple and natural way, you will not fail. Spend the time you have spent in sighing for fruits in fulfilling the conditions of their growth. The fruits will come, must come. We have hitherto paid immense attention to *effects*, to the mere experiences themselves; we have described them, extolled them, advised them, prayed for them—done everything but find out what *caused* them. Henceforth let us deal with causes. " To be," says Lotze, " is to be in relations." About every other method of living the Christian life there is an uncertainty. About every other method of acquiring the Christian experiences there is a " perhaps." But in so far as this method is the way of nature, it cannot fail. Its guarantee is the laws of the universe, and these are " the Hands of the Living God."